HEAT UP
YOUR
COLD
CALLS

How to Make Prospects
Listen, Respond, and Buy

GEORGE R. WALTHER

Dearborn™
Trade Publishing
A **Kaplan Professional** Company

This publication is designed to provide accurate and authoritative information in regard to the subject matter covered. It is sold with the understanding
that the publisher is not engaged in rendering legal, accounting, or other
professional service. If legal advice or other expert assistance is required, the
services of a competent professional person should be sought.

President, Dearborn Publishing: Roy Lipner
Vice President and Publisher: Cynthia A. Zigmund
Acquisitions Editor: Michael Cunningham
Senior Managing Editor: Jack Kiburz
Interior Design: Lucy Jenkins
Cover Design: Scott Rattray, Rattray Design
Typesetting: the dotted i

Published by Dearborn Trade Publishing
A Kaplan Professional Company

Printed in the United States of America

05 06 07 08   10 9 8 7 6 5 4 3 2

Library of Congress Cataloging-in-Publication Data

Walther, George R.
    Heat up your cold calls : how to make prospects listen, respond, and
buy / George R. Walther.
        p.   cm.
    Includes index.
    ISBN 1-4195-0276-X (pbk.)
    1. Telephone selling.   2. Telemarketing.   I. Title.
HF5438.3.W35 2005
658.8′72—dc22
                                                                2004029167

3487434L 4/07

Dearborn Trade books are available at special quantity discounts to use for
sales promotions, employee premiums, or educational purposes. Please call
our Special Sales Department to order or for more information at 800-621-
9621, ext. 4444, e-mail trade@dearborn.com, or write to Dearborn Trade
Publishing, 30 South Wacker Drive, Suite 2500, Chicago, IL 60606-7481.

PRAISE FOR *HEAT UP YOUR COLD CALLS*

"Legendary customer service starts when your customers are your prospects, and George shows you how to start relationships right. If you don't enjoy giving or receiving sales calls, this book is for you! George shows you how to turn your sales pitch into a conversation with your next lifetime customer."

Tim Newsom, manager, Strategic Business Development,
Starbucks Coffee Company

"This powerful, practical, fast-moving book shows you proven ways to get all the qualified prospects you want, fill your sales pipeline, and supercharge your income."

Brian Tracy, author, *The Psychology of Selling*

"George Walther is hot and so is his book. If you cold call and you don't use this book as a bible, you're not only making a big mistake, you're costing yourself big money. Buy it, read it, and use it every day."

Jeffrey Gitomer, author, *The Little Red Book of Selling*

"I HATE cold calls! That's why I LOVE George Walther's newest book, *Heat Up Your Cold Calls*. It provides specific, practical techniques for turning those cold calls into hot prospects."

Dr. Tony Alessandra, author, *Non-Manipulative Selling*
and *The Platinum Rule*

"This is a brilliant program from the country's top expert. Grab it, study it, and benefit enormously."

Nido Qubein, president, High Point University,
and chairman, Great Harvest Bread Company

"Finally, a sales guide that stresses the *ethical* way to deal with prospects and customers. This is the way buying relationships should always begin—with the positive long-run in mind. Walther's book embodies the principles of success."

Jack Canfield, co-creator, *Chicken Soup for the Soul®*,
and author, *The Success Principles™*

"Over the years so much of what has been written about cold calling is outdated or impractical. In his new book, *Heat Up Your Cold Calls*, George Walther brings new and much-needed ideas about the art and science of cold calling. He provides both the philosophy and the practice of warming up prospects fast. If you make cold calls, you absolutely need this book."

Mark Sanborn, speaker and author, *The Fred Factor: How Passion in Your Work and Life Can Make the Ordinary Extraordinary*

"George has nailed the process to turn up the thermostat on those cold calls. He shows you from his many years of experience how to put your reputation on the line ethically and build long-term relationships and achieve results. It doesn't matter whether you are a beginner or an experienced professional in selling. This is a must-read if you want to arrive at your destination ahead of schedule."

Howard Putnam, speaker and author, *The Winds of Turbulence,* and former CEO, Southwest Airlines

"George Walther has done it! He has delivered the sales world a practical, how-to-do-it set of strategies that far supersede any of the outdated, tired ways to prospect and win more business that have been recycled for years. Read this book; it's fantastic!"

William T. Brooks, author, *The New Science of Selling and Persuasion*

"Clients are looking for salespeople they can trust. They want friendly warmth, not cold calls. George Walther is an expert at connecting with people. He has specialized in persuasive communication for decades. Follow his wisdom and add a human touch to your selling. Your customers will be glad you did."

Jim Cathcart, author, *Relationship Selling*

"When it comes to sales knowledge and expertise, George Walther is one of the top pros in the business. *Heat Up Your Cold Calls* reminds successful salespeople how to continue being successful, and teaches beginning salespeople how to become successful."

Michael LeBoeuf, author, *How to Win Customers and Keep Them for Life*

DEDICATION

My work is dedicated to those parents who place their children ahead of all other priorities. As a single father, I know what it takes to put your career on a back burner while you focus on the much more important job of parenting. I particularly acknowledge single parents of both genders who make personal sacrifices for the benefit of their children. Thank you.

OTHER WORKS BY GEORGE R. WALTHER

BOOKS

Phone Power
Power Talking
Upside-Down Marketing
What You Say Is What You Get

VIDEO TRAINING PROGRAMS

Gut-Level Leadership
Phone Power
Positive Practice Communication Tool Kit
Power Talking
Upside-Down Selling
TeleMax

AUDIO TRAINING PROGRAMS

Never Make Another Cold Call
Phone Power (Multiple Editions)
Power Talking
Profitable Telemarketing
TeleMarkeTrends
What You Say Is What You Get
The Power to Please: Delivering Exceptional Customer Service

Contents

PART THREE

Ready, Set, Dial!

PART FOUR

Get Past Those Hang-Ups

The only people who hate cold calls more than the just-sitting-down-for-dinner consumers and the harried-call-dodging businesspeople who receive them are *you*, the sales professionals who have to make them! You and every other salesperson universally dread having to call strangers and attempt to persuade them that they ought to buy something. Convincing them to part with their valuable time when setting appointments for face-to-face sales calls is even more challenging.

Cold calls are extremely unpopular at both ends of the line. True enough, there was a time when salespeople found it profitable to purchase lists of "suspects" and just begin dialing. Indeed, there was even a time when sales managers handed out telephone books or the infamous crisscross listings showing every resident or business on a given street. They instructed their newly recruited salespeople to just start with the *A*s, or to begin calling every number on Main Street.

Cold calls to consumers were the spam of their day. At first, some people actually found it novel and intriguing that complete strangers phoned them in the evening with some sort of pitch. Then, those same consumers became slightly annoyed. Then they got angry. They purchased call-zappers, begged their telephone service providers to have their numbers unlisted, or paid a monthly charge to have the phone company greet all callers with an announcement indicating that unsolicited calls were unwelcome. These measures provided consumers with temporary relief—until sales organizations found clever ways to get around the call-blocking technologies.

Finally, enough people got mad enough that blind cold calls to consumers at home were by and large outlawed. In fact, the Federal Trade Commission's Do Not Call list has become one of the most popular government programs of all time.

Heading off to the office in the morning provided consumers with little relief from unwelcome calls. "Toner-phoners" and various other telemarketing pirates bombarded switchboard operators with often-deceptive canvassing calls hoping to find the individuals responsible for purchasing office supplies or to arrange meetings with CEOs. (You and I still get plenty of these calls.)

Again, the recipients of these unwelcome calls adopted defensive strategies. Secretaries and personal assistants became overzealous in protecting their bosses. Productivity-conscious businesspeople began instructing their secretaries to be highly skeptical of phone calls from individuals whose names they didn't recognize. "Keep them away so I can get something done!" became their rallying cry.

When cold caller salespeople *did* succeed at penetrating screens and actually reached a live person who could even become a sales prospect, they typically encountered a high degree of cynical skepticism.

But what about the other end of the line?

Nothing burns out a fresh new sales professional as much as being given the assignment of placing a series of cold calls. The suspects, who the salesperson hopes will become prospects and eventually customers, don't want to be interrupted with unsolicited sales calls. Cold callers experience an extraordinarily high degree of frustration before they even speak with their suspects.

And if the salesperson is eventually successful at negotiating and penetrating the various obstacles—unhelpful switchboard operators, labyrinth-like voice mail systems, and protective secretaries—that's when the truly negative reaction sets in.

Let's face it; all prospective customers have been burned by sloppy, deceptive, rude, ill-prepared, and downright unprofessional salespeople. They've learned, with good reason, to be skeptical about solicitation calls. So they react with great annoyance when they're interrupted by one.

Rejection! Within just a few days, many a newly recruited salesperson gets fed up, depressed, negative, and ultimately convinced that sales is a lousy career choice.

There is a much better way than traditional cold calling, and that's what this book is all about. You'll be able to adapt and adopt the successful strategies of real-life sales professionals who have found simple yet powerful ways to effectively establish relationships with suspects, who then become prospects and ultimately long-term, delighted customers. By following the specific tips and techniques covered in these pages, you can dramatically reduce the amount of frustration, cynicism, and skepticism you encounter . . . starting today.

That's not to say that this book is magic. I can't give you the golden secret that will create 100 percent success with your cold calling ventures. What I *can* promise is that you'll experience far less rejection and a far higher success rate by using the strategies we'll explore here.

"DO THE RIGHT THING" . . . WHILE YOU BUILD A HIGHLY EFFECTIVE PROSPECTING SYSTEM

Every selling approach advocated in this book is designed to create four positive outcomes:

1. They're good for *you:* The Prospect Preheating System spelled out here will subject you to far less rejection and burnout. You'll experience less fatigue, depression, and disgust. And, of course, you'll experience greater positive results, whether that means scheduling more face-to-face appointments, consummating more and larger

immediate sales, or cultivating longer-term and more highly profitable relationships with new customers.

2. They're good for *your prospects:* The people you call on will be far more pleasant to deal with. They'll recognize that you're being respectful of them and considerate of their time demands. Prospects who really wouldn't be candidates for the services or products you offer will no longer have to deal with your unwelcome attention. At the same time, those prospects who *would* stand to benefit greatly from your attention will get lots more of it.

3. They're good for *your company:* Every business wants to gain the greatest possible return on its invested resources. The prospecting techniques employed by most old-school solicitors are highly wasteful. The *preheating* approach you'll read about here will ensure that your company enjoys much greater leverage. You'll produce more results per expenditure of time and money.

4. They're good for *our industry and profession:* The problems that have plagued business-to-consumer marketers have been self-inflicted. You know it yourself. You've been annoyed at home by unsolicited and unwelcome incoming calls from rude telemarketers who always seemed to reach you just as you were about to enjoy a quiet evening meal with your family. Naturally, consumers eventually spoke up *en masse* and prompted their legislators to take action. The preheating approach in this book ensures the long-term longevity and good reputation of our industry by making sure that only people who may benefit from our attention get it.

HOW THIS BOOK IS ORGANIZED

You can certainly skip around to the chapters that seem most relevant to the challenges you're facing right now, but you'll also find that this book is organized with a logical flow through five major parts:

Part 1. We'll start with a solid foundation and explore why you shouldn't ever make another cold call. Sure, the legal landscape has become prohibitive for many types of calls. There's something even more important, however, than legal restrictions: *cold calls rarely work!* I'm certainly not advocating that you should never call new, unfamiliar prospects . . . only that you should never call them *cold.*

Part 2. The fundamental concept of this whole book is that you're much better off taking sensible steps before your call to ensure that your prospects are preheated. We'll talk about how to employ your most powerful ally, your pre-existing relationship. Even though you might not think you have one, I'll show you how to create it. Before you pick up your phone, we need to perform a little brain surgery and then make sure your head and your mouth are in sync to create the positive outcomes you seek.

Part 3. Calls that produce positive results don't happen by accident. There's a logic to them. In fact, I'll break the effective call into its five logical phases. I'll guide you through the five parts of a successful call and show you, with real-life examples from a wide range of industries, exactly how each phase moves you toward success.

Part 4. Now, we'll put it all into practice and focus on "special situations." Whether you're phoning to schedule appointments or create immediate sales, we have to understand how your prospects decide to say yes. Of course, not all of them will. So it's important to see how we can snatch victories from what look like defeats. You'll want your skills to improve over time, so I'll show you exactly how to track and improve your effectiveness.

Part 5. This is only the beginning! You'll probably reread this book often and return to the chapters that are most helpful for you. In this concluding section, you find many additional resources, including an extensive online appendix and specific suggestions for staying on the path of continual improvement.

Each chapter begins with a quick preview, so you'll know what lies just ahead. Because the underlying aim of this book is to help you take action, every chapter concludes with a bulleted list of steps you can take to put these ideas into practice immediately.

Now, let's dive right in . . . and make sure the water's not too chilly.

GETTING AHEAD IN A DO NOT CALL WORLD

Everything starts in your head. The sales landscape has changed dramatically in the last few years, and you've got to change the way you think about it, too. The old way of cold calling just doesn't cut it anymore. Your return on investment from just power dialing through lists of names would be pitiful, even if you were willing to work for peanuts. And even if you were, you'd end up in the clinker unless you were very, very careful to tiptoe through the new legal minefield out there.

You don't *want* to make cold calls, you *shouldn't* make them, and you don't *have to* make them. In fact, you'd be dumb (and get arrested) doing things the way salespeople used to.

1

NEVER MAKE ANOTHER COLD CALL!

What we'll cover in Chapter 1:

- Why you should change your vocabulary and your thoughts to eliminate the term *cold call*
- The concept of *preheating* your prospects
- The *conveyor belt analogy* that helps to keep the big picture in mind, so you know where your prospecting efforts fit in the overall scheme of business
- The relative costs and rewards of the three essential marketing functions: *recruiting, retaining, and recapturing customers*

That's right! I urge you to never make another *cold* call. I'm talking about cold calls in the traditional sense—the kind that rookie salespeople have made for years, and the kind that have alienated customers and created a bad reputation for the whole selling profession. These old-fashioned cold calls have also been responsible for the premature burnout of talented communicators who might well have developed into superb professional salespeople if they had not become so disgusted with the whole cold-calling process that they cut short the learning curve and bailed out.

It will always be necessary to initiate contact with prospective customers, and that's exactly what this book will show you how to do. But we won't use the approaches that were accepted, commonplace practice for years. And with good reason. Their effectiveness has dwindled, and they've been getting us into trouble.

DON'T SAY (OR EVEN THINK) "COLD"

What you say shapes how you think, which affects your actions. Everybody hates *cold calls* (making or receiving them), so don't put yourself in that frame of mind by even using the term. It spells certain self-sabotage. Later in this book, we explore more thoroughly the impact that specific words and phrases have on your thoughts and actions. For now, let me just put it like this: If you reach for your phone and say you're about to make a cold call, you're programming yourself to expect a chilly reception. This puts you in a defensive posture. Your word choices and vocal profile communicate your underlying attitudes to your prospects. When you describe your call as cold, you think of it that way and act accordingly. This book is all about how to make an entirely different and far more productive type of call: the prospect preheating call.

I'm going to show you how to ensure that your prospect is warmed up before you dial. This puts you in a more confident, positive frame of mind. When you feel better, you sound better. So using a more positive vocabulary and being in a better frame of mind, you produce more positive results.

QUIT TREATING PROSPECTS LIKE PASTA

One of Peter Drucker's most useful contributions to the lexicon of business is his clear differentiation between the words *efficiency* and *effectiveness.* Efficiency is *doing things right.* Effectiveness, Drucker reminds us, is *doing the right things.* Balancing the two is a major challenge in any commercial enterprise, particularly when it comes to prospecting.

The folly of most sales-prospecting activities is that they are both inefficient and ineffective. Salespeople often employ the *al dente* approach familiar to pasta chefs everywhere. Fling a lot of noodles (or leads) at the wall or ceiling and see if some stick. When some do, you've succeeded! The pasta is ready; you've got a prospect! If nothing sticks, keep flinging more and more up there until something sticks and your efforts pay off. You've just got to make more calls, the conventional wisdom taught.

Most marketers pursue a large number of potential leads, send out heaps of costly sales literature, schedule many face-to-face sales calls, and clog up their appointment calendar with multiple phone contacts. Most of this attention goes to leads that are often completely unqualified. Very few are likely to ever buy anything and should really be thought of only as suspects. Sales managers often justify this wasteful approach by saying, "Prospecting is just a numbers game. Make lots of calls, and something is bound to happen."

The pasta chef's approach results in salespeople who are so busy chasing all those unqualified leads that they fail to give quality attention to the relatively few leads who might actually become qualified prospects.

SEEK RELATIONSHIPS, NOT SALES

In my sales and marketing keynote presentations to corporations and associations worldwide, one of the most important concepts I explain is what I call the "conveyor belt analogy." It goes like this: I arrange two long banquet tables on the stage and place them end-to-end. From your perspective in the audience, you see a single 12-foot-long narrow table on the stage. I ask you to imagine that you're not seeing a long table, but instead visualize the beginning portion of an infinitely long conveyor belt. Your success in business is measured by the number of customers you can persuade to get on, *and remain on,* your conveyor belt. This is because, over time, their repeat future transactions become increasingly profitable. When it comes to cold calling, your most profitable course of action is to seek customers who are most likely to remain on your belt for a long time.

KEEP THE BIG PICTURE IN FOCUS

Even if *your* primary responsibility is restricted to prospecting, it's still well worth your while to understand the big picture of marketing to ensure that your efforts are focused on producing the kinds of customers who will generate the greatest and most profitable returns.

The least profitable sale you can ever make is the first one to a new customer. That's because any profit from the first transaction is overshadowed by the marketing cost of getting the customer on the relationship conveyor belt in the first place. In marketing terms, this is referred to as the "acquisition cost."

Let's suppose that you make nine unsuccessful no-sale calls. Then, jackpot! Your prospecting efforts finally result in one new customer who makes a $1,000 purchase from you. If you have a gross profit margin of 20 percent, that means you expect to enjoy a $200 profit. Let's be very conservative and estimate that when all expenses are considered, your cost to reach each prospective customer is only $50. (In actuality it's often far, far higher when you account for advertising costs, sales department overhead, phones, equipment, computer costs, staffing expenses, and so on.) Still, you might say, "When you close a $1,000 sale with a $200 profit, and it cost just $50 to gain this customer, that's not so bad."

Hold everything! What about the nine people who said no before this one said yes? The true marketing cost to acquire the customer who said yes must include all the other marketing efforts that were *un*successful. So we're really talking about a marketing expense of all ten customer contacts at $50 each, or $500 (recognizing that this is an unrealistically conservative figure for most business scenarios). What happened to your $200 profit? Actually, you lost money!

Even though it's absolutely necessary to acquire, or "recruit," new customers, it's just not profitable to do so in the short run. You need a new, more effective, and more efficient way to cold call. You must ensure that your prospecting attention focuses on customers with a high likelihood of buying and continuing to buy.

When I'm on a stage demonstrating this principle for an audience, I step up on the banquet tables (or imaginary conveyor belt) and jump for joy, because that's what most salespeople do when they win a new customer. They get excited and start anticipating how they'll spend their commission. I want us all to recognize that the process of acquiring new customers is not profitable. It's just *necessary*. It's only the first step in creating relationships that can later become profitable.

Fortunately, there is a real opportunity for profits that results from keeping customers on that conveyor belt—that is, retaining them—because all future transactions contribute incrementally more to your bottom-line profit. The initial acquisition cost to win a new customer is amortized over future transactions so they yield more profits. The cost of recruiting the customer in the first place is now in the distant past.

Keeping customers on the conveyor belt, retaining their long-term loyalty in your buying-selling relationship, is what yields profit. This task is normally relegated to the Customer Service

Department, which has historically been viewed as a cost center rather than a profit center. Fortunately, we've been in an age of enlightenment the last couple of decades. Sales organizations have come to realize that retaining, or hanging on to, customers is actually more profitable than recruiting them—that is, getting them on the conveyor belt in the first place.

Most sales professionals reading this book have a compelling vested interest in nurturing their customers' relationships well beyond the initial solicitation calls. Retention pays off. You may be directly rewarded with commissions from ongoing revenue streams of customers whose relationships you brought to life. Or you may be working in an organization where that's someone else's responsibility. Your livelihood is always dependent on your company's being profitable and successful. So get bigger returns on your investments of time and energy by allocating more of your attention to existing customers. Calling them not only helps to ensure their long-term loyalty and ongoing revenue stream, it also provides tremendous personal benefits to you.

When it comes to your role in the prospecting stage, it's very much in your best interest (and your company's) to focus on finding and preheating prospective customers who are likely to not just buy . . . you want customers who are likely to *keep on* buying.

By calling to nurture and retain satisfied customers, you are continually reenergized and reminded of why your customers like to do business with you. This reaffirmation of your organization's worth helps you project genuine enthusiasm to prospective new customers, those who have not yet made the decision to climb aboard. In the course of contacting current customers to nurture their relationships, you're bound to encounter testimonials from people who feel very happy about doing business with you. These you can pass along to prospective customers who have not yet had the opportunity to see how beneficial their relationship with you will become.

There is actually a third task in marketing that's even more profitable than recruiting and retention: remedying defections.

The most costly event that can occur in a customer relationship is the loss of an active, profitable account. Even though we focus a lot of attention on customers who make a big noise and call to curse us, write letters to the company president, and very vocally denounce our organizations, those noisily disgruntled customers represent only a very small percentage of customers whose loyalty fades over time.

One of the world's biggest computer companies once retained me to help train an elite squad of marketers whose job it was to handle customers who had written "Lew Letters." The CEO, named Lew, received letters from the most disgruntled, complaining customers. They were eventually forwarded to his office for special attention. In turn, they ultimately made their way to this special team of telephone professionals in one of the mountain states.

As I sat with these highly skilled individuals, I reviewed with them the history of each customer's correspondence before making individual calls. Here's what most amazed me: In instance after instance, the customers we were about to call had registered their dissatisfaction much earlier without getting prompt and appropriate attention. They had stewed for a while until their dissatisfaction had escalated; by the time they wrote to the CEO, weeks had often passed. And by the time the executive office eventually sent their cases to the complaint squad, *months* had passed! The longer you wait to please or placate dissatisfied customers, the more difficult it is to do. During the months these unhappy customers had been waiting for appropriate attention, what do you think they'd been doing? They certainly *weren't* buying products from the company. And they certainly *weren't* telling their colleagues how much they respected the company and its products. How much expense and negative publicity could have been saved had the original salesperson responsible for the customers' satisfaction taken the reins and made sure that the complaints were handled promptly?

Even though we eventually pay a lot of attention to the most vocal complainers, the leading cause of customer defections is quiet neglect. Although it's beyond the scope of this book to discuss in detail, the most profitable thing you can do in marketing is to remedy the "defection disease" and win back unhappy customers. The sooner the better.

There are three big reasons why: First, you're very likely to regain the customer's business if you quickly use the proper approach. Second, a defecting customer can tell you exactly what factors drove him or her away. If there's some deficiency in your marketing and fulfillment system, the people who can best identify it are those who became so fed up that they were motivated to stop doing business with you. Third, with proper attention you can perhaps defuse ex-customers' ire. At least you'll silence some of their criticism and thus alleviate much of their bad-mouthing your organization in the marketplace. In all likelihood, you can actually create positive press if you do an outstanding job of solving customers' complaints.

If the least profitable, but crucially important, task in any selling relationship is recruiting or acquiring the customer in the first place, it's no wonder that it's worth your expending such effort to prospect both efficiently and effectively.

Your whole cold calling mind-set has to change. If your firm's eventual success and profitability result from its ability to keep customers on your conveyor belt for many repeat purchases, then you should be prospecting for *relationships*, not sales. A marketing campaign that pulls in 10,000 onetime buyers is much less profitable than one that produces 2,500 four-time buyers who have the potential for remaining active customers for years.

As you design and modify your prospecting system, your goal should *not* be to produce leads or even sales. Your aim should be to produce leads that turn into sales *that turn into relationships*. Every time you produce a lead that doesn't go on to become a sale and a long-term relationship, you're costing your company money, not producing profits.

Heat Up Your Cold Calls focuses on the most difficult phase of any customer relationship: the beginning. It's also the most costly. In many organizations, a huge amount of resources is dedicated to developing lots and lots of prospective new customer leads. It's easy to measure the *quantity* of your lead-generation results. Keep in mind, though, that having lots of leads means little. A high volume may actually be counterproductive. As long as the number of leads is easy to measure, though, leads will be the rewarded goal of prospecting systems. Stop measuring the quantity of leads you generate; focus on the *quality* of the results you produce.

W*hat you can do, starting NOW:*

- Purge cold calling from your vocabulary and your thoughts.
- Focus your prospecting efforts on individuals who are likely to continue buying after the initial sale.
- Check back with your existing customers to nurture and help retain their buying relationships, even if it's not formally part of your job.
- Incorporate the happy-customer testimonials you hear into your prospecting efforts.
- Whenever you encounter unhappy/dissatisfied customers, do all you can to facilitate rapid resolution of their concerns. You don't want them to bad-mouth you to future prospects.
- Shift your focus from gathering a high quantity of leads to homing in on high-*quality* leads who are likely to begin long-term buying relationships.

2

"DO NOT CALL" . . .
DEAL WITH IT!

What we'll cover in Chapter 2:

- Knowing what you *must not do* to avoid harsh penalties as a result of recent laws that are changing constantly and that severely limit traditional cold calling activity
- Important exceptions that allow you to contact consumers at home in specific situations
- How maintaining active business relationships can protect you from restrictions
- How thinking long term can protect you, your company, and our profession from severe penalties and negative impacts

The last thing you want to do is end up in hot water (or in jail) just because you were seeking prospective customers. The fact is that the old-fashioned way of placing cold calls is now illegal in many instances. You can not only get yourself into a lot of trouble, you can also literally put your company out of business if you run afoul of the laws governing prospecting activity.

Let me go on the record to assure you that I'm not an attorney and am not offering any legal advice in this book. I have reviewed the Federal Trade Commission's Telemarketing Sales Rule and this legislation's most noteworthy amendment, the National Do Not Call Registry. I can guarantee that *you* definitely don't want to read those whopping documents! There are, though, a number of private companies that will assist your firm and help you stay on the right side of the law. For a current listing, check this book's online appendix at http://www .HeatUpYourColdCalls.com. It's vital to understand that both state and federal legislators have a lot to say about your calling activities. And what they have to say changes. It's critical that you check the Internet and verify the current legislation that applies to your particular state. A good starting point for the national legislation is the government Web site http://www .DoNotCall.gov. Various state rules have an impact on the hours you may call, what you may say in the first few seconds of the call, what sort of relationship must preexist with your potential customer, and so on.

THE LAW TRANSLATED TO MARKETERS' EVERYDAY LANGUAGE

In response to the great public outcry expressing frustration and annoyance about unsolicited calls from telemarketers, the Federal Trade Commission amended the Telephone Sales Rule and established the National Do Not Call Registry in 2003. This legislation gives all consumers the right to notify marketers that they do not wish to receive sales calls. You'd better pay attention. The initial fine for phoning a consumer who has registered on the Do Not Call list can be $11,000 *per violation!*

Don't make the mistake of thinking that you can ignore all these complicated regulations if you're "just a little guy." You can't! It's even more important for independent operators to stay abreast of, and comply with, the laws. Large corporations with huge sales organizations can afford to have lawyers and lobbyists constantly monitoring the situation. Independents can't. A few large fines might hurt big companies, but they won't close down a big multinational sales organization. For a small or medium company, a series of violations (at $11,000 a pop) can mean bankruptcy.

If you're an *individual* whose livelihood stems from direct selling, a couple of missteps that lead to complaints can put you out of business in a hurry. Be sure you regularly refer to the Web site linked to this book: http://www.HeatUpYourColdCalls.com. It provides you with legislative updates and cross-references other sites that will lead you to your state's legislative summaries.

There are some very important exceptions to the cold calling restrictions: Nonprofit organizations calling for fundraising purposes, survey companies such as pollsters and market research firms, and political entities are all exempt from the regulations. In the business world, the most important exception is that a firm may contact anyone with whom it has had business dealings in the last 18 months, even if that person is registered on the Do Not Call list. The legislation specifically notes that the business relationship is deemed to exist if the consumer has had a "purchase, delivery, or payment" within a year and a half.

NO "GET-OUT-OF-JAIL-FREE" CARDS IN THIS GAME

One consistent theme throughout this book is that you reap your greatest rewards when you keep the big picture in focus and think long term. That same advice applies in the area of penalties just as it does with rewards.

When it comes to legal penalties, most people are concerned about being fined for mistakenly calling someone who is on the Do Not Call list and files a complaint. Yes, an $11,000 penalty can certainly hurt, especially if you've made dozens or hundreds of these calls and then have to pay the price. But protect yourself by thinking beyond the monetary value of the fines themselves and focusing on some of the bigger problems that could result for you or your company.

Your Firm's Future Is at Stake, Not to Mention Your Career

If your marketing organization repeatedly runs afoul of federal or state laws, you can put yourself out of business. That's not just because the fines can mount to astronomical levels very quickly; it's also because of negative publicity. Suppose the *Wall Street Journal* runs an article about unscrupulous marketers who flaunt legal restrictions, and your firm is cited as an example? What would *that* do to your company? How do you suppose your career path would be affected if you were the one who decided you didn't really need to heed every little detail of the legislation?

Long Term, It's Suicidal for the Sales Profession

Let's think even bigger, though. It's not just about you and it's not just about your company. What about our profession? Over the long haul, the entire marketing industry is affected by your personal actions. The genesis for these restrictive laws was the actions of some shortsighted individuals. Enough "bad guys" called consumers at home late in the evening, concealed who they were and why they were calling, and then rudely hung up when the person they phoned didn't want to buy. Consumers' collective hue and cry led directly to the current state of affairs. Please, do yourself, your company, your industry, and our whole profession a favor: Know the law. Abide by the law. And go well beyond the law by using common sense and simply treating your prospective customers with respect and common courtesy.

HOW THE BUSINESS-TO-CONSUMER AND BUSINESS-TO-BUSINESS MARKETS DIFFER

As a practical matter, the restrictive legislation is designed primarily to protect consumers at home. That does not mean that business calls are exempt from regulation, however. Once again, it's critical that you verify legislation affecting your particular state and industry. You or somebody in your organization should maintain an active membership in your professional association, such as those listed in this book's online appendix. Not only are there compelling reasons to remain current with legislative restrictions, but industry gatherings also keep you abreast of technological innovations and allow you to share the "best practices" employed by your competitors! Make it a point to have someone in your organization attend industry events each year. You can rub shoulders not just with those who are in your direct line of business but also meet top-level professionals who journey from dozens of countries around the world and contribute their ideas to this global marketers' brain trust. For details about associations and upcoming gatherings, visit the links listed at http://www.HeatUpYourColdCalls.com. Don't assume because you're calling people at their place of business, you don't have to worry about restrictive legislation.

THERE'S NO QUICKER WAY TO BURNOUT THAN CALLING COLD

Frustration, rejection, wheel spinning, and self-doubt are guaranteed to cold callers. True enough, there are some salespeople who claim they relish the opportunity to jump on the phone and start pounding out calls to unqualified leads. Personally, I always thought these people had a few screws loose.

Simply put, there's just no argument in favor of making the traditional type of cold calls. They're quite often illegal. They can get you into big trouble. They're not profitable. Start calling people with whom you have no demonstrated connection, and you're sure to experience very high levels of frustration and rejection. You get burned out and lose any momentum you might have had at the start of your sales career.

I implore you to *never make another cold call.* Instead, implement the preheating strategies you'll find in the following chapters and employ the strategies and tactics we'll cover in the pages ahead. They will keep you out of trouble and squarely on the path toward a productive and profitable use of your prospecting resources.

W *hat you can do, starting NOW:*

- Keep up-to-date with current sales laws by visiting http://www .HeatUpYourColdCalls.com.
- Maintain customer transaction frequency intervals shorter than 18 months to keep your legal exemptions valid.
- Be an active member in professional associations to stay abreast of regulatory impacts on your particular industry.
- Make plans to attend your industry's trade shows and association meetings so you can rub shoulders with colleagues and exchange ideas about legal, ethical prospecting methods.

PREHEAT YOUR PROSPECTS

If you're not going to call prospects cold, how can you heat them up? Your two very best tools are your preexisting relationships and your manner of speaking (and thinking) as you approach that initial contact.

If you're thinking, "But, I don't have a preexisting relationship with my prospect," you're most likely wrong! If you truly have none at all, you shouldn't be making the call. With a little creativity, though, we can identify the relationship, even though it's not obvious. And we'll put it to good use!

How you think and what you say . . . and do . . . are all connected. Let's make sure that your words, thoughts, and actions take full advantage of the relationship you've discovered or created.

3

SIMPLE STEPS TO WARM UP YOUR COLD CALLS

What we'll cover in Chapter 3:

- The beginning of establishing trust with your prospects by relying on your most powerful tool: your relationship
- Mastering the ascending levels of power on the relationship ladder: perceived affinity groups, formal memberships, implied referrals, and named referrals
- Learning how to create a perceived affinity group even when you don't think one exists
- Benefiting from seminars and speaking opportunities that position you as a qualified expert in your field
- Writing and publishing articles and brochures to build your credibility
- Using e-mail to warm up your prospects without being perceived as a spammer
- Using the Internet to research your prospects before you make the call
- Old-fashioned communications that, ironically, become more and more valuable in preheating your prospects

Before you make your very first contact with a stranger, the atmosphere is certainly cold. You want your prospect to feel warm about you to increase the likelihood that you'll be successful in capturing your prospect's attention and establishing rapport. You want to preheat your prospects.

RELATIONSHIPS OPEN THE DOORS

Your ultimate goal in just about any sales scenario is to develop a long-term buying relationship with your prospects. If you work for a company that only wants you to open accounts, nurturing prospects may be delegated to someone else. Still, your firm's (and your) long-term success depends on your ability to at least get the relationship started right. The long-term relationship is the endgame, where the most profits are to be gained and the easiest sales take place. A long-term, trust-based partnership is the ideal scenario. You want your customer to exhibit allegiance toward you and your company, and you will earn that allegiance only by becoming viewed as a trusted partner. But that's way down the line. For now, we need to establish the foundation, and that begins with your very first contact.

Your prospects are pressured, rushed, and often quite cynical. It's understandable they would be reluctant to trust you right away. So your primary challenge at the start of any cold call is to establish a basis for trust. And your number one tool for doing that is your preexisting relationship, even if you have to create it.

CLIMB UP THE RELATIONSHIP LADDER

There are several possible levels of relationship value. You can think of them as a sort of hierarchy or ladder. Because you face the daunting task of gaining prospects' trust up front, it behooves you to start as high on that ladder as you can possibly get.

If a complete stranger comes a-knockin' on your door . . . or buzzes the intercom for your high-rise . . . will you let this unknown person in? Probably not. Even beyond your sensible concern for personal security, you don't want to give up your time to someone who may turn out to be a complete waste or, even worse, a rude imposition.

However, if a member of your neighborhood association, of which you are also a member, rings you to ask a favor, you'll be much more likely to talk to this person rather than to a stranger. And if you are contacted by a good friend of a good friend of yours, you'll almost certainly talk to this person.

All of us make decisions about whom we'll spend time with based on a relationship hierarchy. One of the biggest troubles with a true cold call in the classic sense is that you have started as low as you can go on the relationship ladder. The very bottom rung is where you put people when they have no demonstrated connection to you; they're strangers. You won't answer the door for them, buzz them up to your unit, meet with them in your office, or even take time to talk with them on the phone.

Because one of your first goals when contacting prospective customers is to capture and hold their attention, you've got to make sure that you get to the highest rung you can manage on that relationship ladder as fast as you can.

If "complete stranger" is the lowest rung on the ladder, what are the ascending rungs you can climb?

Create Your Own Perceived Affinity Groups

Ever heard of a perceived affinity group? A membership affinity group, of course, is a collection of individuals who share a common interest, often with formal membership. Maybe they are all members of a dog breeder's association, purchasing agents in a particular industry, people sharing a common profession, or perhaps those with a geographic connection. *Perceived* indicates that the group doesn't truly exist in a formal sense. Yet the person who shares these common interests, on hearing a description of such a hypothetical group, would conclude: "That sounds like it's for me! Those are my interests."

One of the crucial keys to your prospecting success is your ability to *create* perceived affinity groups. If you were given the job of generating leads for sales of window covering systems, you'd have much less success canvassing from some alphabetical directory than you would if you concentrated your attention on a specific market niche. If you're going to develop expertise in a specialized niche, though, say so!

> "Mrs. Cotter, my specialty is helping homeowners on the east shore of Bear Lake with their window treatments. Afternoon sun reflections off the lake create special challenges, as you've noticed, and I've been able to source some innovative new materials for blinds and drapes that do a great job handling your conditions."

You set yourself apart from the generic window treatment salesperson by introducing yourself as an individual with special expertise that this prospective customer should want to take advantage of. If there actually were a club, or affinity group, for people who live on the east side of Bear Lake and who deal with the sun beating down on their conventional window blinds, your prospect would qualify for membership.

In a formal sense, though, the club doesn't exist. So you create it—hypothetically, at least. Don't get me wrong now. I'm not advocating any dishonesty and certainly am not suggesting that you say such a club really exists. But you can use the imaginary membership criteria to your advantage. Once you know the common problems that owners of those Bear Lake homes share, you can get busy providing solutions.

This is what I mean by creating a *perceived* affinity group. Figure out what kind of customer would most value your help, find out what that type of customer cares about, develop your expertise in that area, and become a specialist at solving the specific issues those affinity group members share.

Perceived Affinity Groups in Real Estate

One of the most common scenarios in real estate is the seller who lists a home for sale at an unrealistically high (and perhaps greedy) price, thinking that you can always go lower, but you can't go higher. Commonly, sellers interview several real estate agents and often end up listing their home with the agent who estimated the highest sale value, even though it may not have been a realistic estimate.

Typically, other savvy real estate agents recognize that the home is overpriced and don't give it much attention. The excitement that a new listing might normally stir quickly wanes, and the home languishes on the market, creating the impression that the house is "a dog property that just won't sell."

Any marketing momentum the home may have experienced early on quickly fades. The seller hears little from the agent and begins to become disenchanted with the whole selling process. As the listing approaches its expiration date, the real estate agent finally tells the seller it's time to renew the listing. By now, the seller wants nothing to do with the real estate agent and may be disgusted with the whole situation.

One Seattle area real estate agent, Don Burton, used exactly this situation to his advantage by creating a perceived affinity group and becoming an expert in handling expired listings. Today, Don is president of a leading regional mortgage banker, Evergreen Moneysource. In the 1970s, though, he was a brand-new real estate agent looking for ways to set himself apart from the crowded field of more experienced agents. He decided that expired listings offered him a great opportunity.

All real estate agents have access to the Multiple Listing Service database, which shows listings that are about to expire. Once they appeared in the database, Don simply phoned the homeowners and began like this:

> "Dr. Taylor, I've been watching the marketing activity on your home, and I've noticed that it seems to have lost momentum. I specialize in helping West Seattle homeowners market their houses after the initial momentum has begun to fade away. These homeowners I've helped have had great success selling their houses even after they've been on the market with little activity for a long time, as I noticed is the case with your house. May I ask, are you still interested in selling your home?"

At this point, Don braced himself because he typically heard curses denouncing real estate agents. It's no wonder. The sellers didn't sell their home at the price they were led to believe they could expect and typically received very little communication from their listing agents until the listings were about to expire.

When he began to hear the criticisms, Don opened the floodgates by saying, "It sounds like you may have had a negative experience. Would you tell me more about it?" Did they ever! Even though a homeowner had had a negative experience with a previous real estate agent, Don was extraordinarily successful at listing and eventually selling these originally overpriced properties.

Let's see what he did to create this success:

First, he concentrated on highly prequalified leads. He was phoning individuals who had already made the decision to sell their home. That's why they had listed it in the first place.

Right up front, Don concentrated on positioning himself as an expert. He not only focused his expertise on individuals whose listings had expired; he even fine-tuned it geographically, explaining to the homeowners that West Seattle was the area where he specialized. He created a perceived affinity group and then demonstrated his special skill at helping its members.

In his initial contact, Don focused on asking questions and thoroughly and patiently listening to the homeowners' answers. (Read more about questioning strategies in Chapters 8 and 13.) Rather than launching into some long boast to convince them that he was better than any other agent, Don *listened* to the homeowners' concerns.

He let his prospects know that he had done his homework. Don thoroughly familiarized himself with each expired listing before contacting the homeowners. This let them know, early in their conversation, that Don was paying attention and investing the effort necessary to earn their trust.

And of overriding importance, Don let the prospective customers tell him the factors that were of paramount concern to them. When he asked the homeowners to talk about their negative experiences, their most common response was that they had heard very little from the previous listing agent. So Don took advantage of this concern by presetting biweekly appointments with the homeowners. If you had had negative experiences with real estate agents who didn't keep you updated on the progress of your sale, wouldn't you likely respond very favorably when a new listing agent started right off by saying: "I want to make sure we remain in close contact. Let's both check our calendars right now and schedule a meeting every two weeks so I can update you on your marketing activity. Would Wednesday afternoons at three o'clock work for you?"

Memberships Get You Connected

One reason civic organizations, Rotary Clubs, Kiwanis Clubs, and similar groups provide great payoffs to their members is that they foster common bonds. They provide a presumption of trust among members. If you're calling members of your own country club, for example, it's likely that the doors will swing right open and your calls won't be cold. These are affinity groups that exist in a formal sense. You didn't create them.

You don't actually need to be a member of an organization yourself to take great advantage of its membership list though. If you were selling home security systems, and a member of a local homeowners association shared the membership list with you, you'd be able to begin your prospecting calls by indicating that you've been able to help other members of the association.

Caution! Be very careful that you're using the membership list with permission and complying with the organization's usage guidelines. Many organizations have specific policies that prohibit solicitations to their member lists. If you abuse their rules, you immediately put yourself behind the eight ball and aren't likely to get far with your prospecting efforts. What you *are* likely to do is create trouble for yourself.

Using the membership list for an organization of which you're not a member is not necessarily an ethical violation, however. A homeowners association, for example, may give selected vendors permission to use the list, provided that they offer members a significant discount or other benefits. It's also quite possible that the group will require a contributed percentage of your sales to benefit the association, which may be referred to as "revenue sharing" or "nondues revenue programs." Don't be afraid to ask.

If you're using a membership list with permission, be sure to say so at the outset:

> "Mr. Irving, I'm calling you and your neighbors because the Eaglecrest Homeowners Association has arranged for all association members to receive exclusive discounts on home security systems that improve living conditions in the neighborhood. I'm sure you know

Larry Sanchez, the president of your association, and I'm calling with his specific permission."

Implied Referrals Raise You a Rung

If you've installed a security system for Dave Cotter's family, and the Cotters are happy with your work, you can refer to their buying relationship as an "implied referral." Your smartest move, of course, would be to ask the Cotters for permission to use them as a named referral source. Even if you don't have explicit permission, though, invoking their name will still move you a couple of rungs up the relationship ladder from the lowest complete stranger position:

"I've been helping many of your Eaglecrest neighbors protect their homes. In fact, we just completed an installation for the Cotters and they're very pleased with the results. I'd be happy to conduct a security audit for your residence and find out whether a system like the Cotters installed would be just right for your house. I will at the very least be able to advise you on the type of system that would work best for you."

Named Referrals Get You to the Top

The very strongest position you can be in is using a named referral with explicit permission. Because this is such a powerful position, it's well worth your energy to ask current customers for referrals, a particularly valuable topic covered in Chapter 4. For example:

"I've just completed the installation of a comprehensive security system for the Cotter family, your neighbors on View Drive, and I asked Dave which of his neighbors shared his appreciation for the very best in technology. He told me a little bit about your work in high-tech companies and suggested I give you a call."

When it comes to preheating your prospects to avoid encountering a chilly reception, there's no more powerful asset in your arsenal of techniques than a preexisting relationship.

SPEAK OUT AND HEAT THEM UP

As an active member of the National Speakers Association (NSA), I can assure you that presenting public seminars is a great way to warm up prospective customers. Many members, like me, are professional speakers regularly hired by corporations and associations because of our abilities to present profit-producing concepts in a motivating manner. But plenty of other NSA members are not in it for the speaking fees. They seek platform opportunities because they know that audience members perceive the individual at the front of the room to be somebody who has earned the right to address topics as a result of his or her professional expertise. That's a perfect way to warm them up before you make direct personal contact.

Let's suppose you're a wedding planner, and the ideal prospect for your services is an engaged couple that needs help in putting together an event of a lifetime. Why not gather a lineup of cooperating colleagues and present a seminar? You can share the expenses with a photographer, florist, formal wear rental shop owner, department store bridal registry manager, and so on. Rent a hotel ballroom and advertise your event as a seminar on "How to Plan Your Perfect Wedding." All the individuals who register for the event are highly prequalified. They're not going to come to the seminar unless they're in the process of planning their wedding, and that means they need what you sell.

When you contact participants based on their registration information, your call is anything but cold. If you suffer from stage fright, get over it! Join your local Toastmasters group or find out if there's a local chapter of the National Speakers Association you can join. Visit its Web site at http://www.NSAspeaker.org and take advantage of the resources available in your community.

ESTABLISH YOUR CREDIBILITY WITH ARTICLES AND PAMPHLETS

One of the most basic buying motivations is finding solutions to problems, particularly in the business-to-business marketplace. So it stands to reason that buyers will give preference to sellers who have already established and demonstrated their expertise in solving the buyers' specific types of problems. Of course, it would be fantastic if you were widely recognized as a national authority on the topic and appeared frequently on the TV show *Today*. Realistically, though, that's quite unlikely for most of us.

You can, however, create the perception of expertise by taking one very simple step: write! I'm always surprised that people afford so much respect to those who write. One of the most frequent questions I'm asked by my audience members is, "How did you ever manage to write a book?" It's very simple: You think about the value you can offer and what you want to say and then start writing. There's no magic to being a writer. You just sit down and do it.

You're probably much more interested in selling than writing and may even consider yourself a poor writer. But what if doing a little writing, and getting some help to improve your writing, made it much easier for you to sell? It will!

Suppose you're a mortgage broker specializing in helping homeowners refinance their property. Why not write a simple pamphlet titled "The Six Most Common Mistakes Homeowners

Make When They Refinance." Or "How to Determine Whether Refinancing Will Save You Money."

If you sell computer repair services, put together a little pamphlet titled "11 Computer Glitches You Can Fix Yourself . . . and How to Determine When You Need Professional Help."

If you sell corporate travel services, write a practical article on "Five Simple Ways to Increase Your Chances of Being Upgraded to First Class."

Better yet, create a *series* of brief articles or pamphlets. You're not out to create the unrivaled and exhaustive manuscript on your topic. You simply want something tangible that demonstrates your expertise again and again.

For best results, make it short and simple enough to be read right away. Make the content valuable enough that your prospects will hang on to it. Be sure that everything carries your identification and makes it easy for prospects to reach you.

There are at least four good ways to gain mileage and value from such a simple writing project:

1. Preestablish your credibility and familiarity with prospects by sending them your written information *before* you reach out to make personal contact. Ideally, each of your submissions should include a cover letter letting your prospect know when you will be calling.
2. Refer to your pamphlet during the conversation with your prospect. Odds are that this individual has misplaced what you sent, never even saw it, or, at the very least, does not have it readily at hand. This presents a perfect opportunity to direct prospects to your Web site, where they can open, read, and print out what you've written. Get them involved with you.
3. Your pamphlet also gives you a valid reason for scheduling a follow-up call. When you reach a prospect at an inconvenient time, you lessen your chance of success each time you reschedule the call without a specific reason.

You're much better off and much more likely to catch the prospect's attention when you say: "With the amount of mail you and I both get, I'm not a bit surprised that the airline upgrade pamphlet I sent you isn't right there at your fingertips. To save you the trouble of hunting for it, I'm going to send an additional copy, and I'll make a note about our conversation in big bold red ink on the outside of the envelope. Let's plan to talk next Tuesday, and I'll clarify the third and fourth upgrade tips for you then. Is 10:30 in the morning a good time to reach you on Tuesday, or shall I make it right after lunch?"

4. Your tangible written material also makes a perfect follow-up mailing. Even if your prospect's needs don't perfectly match the solutions you offer, send the pamphlet anyway with a cover note expressing appreciation for your prospect's time and suggesting that he or she pass it along to an individual who may need what you offer.

PERIODICALS CAN BREAK THE ICE

If you're going to go to the trouble of writing articles or pamphlets, why not try to have them published? This is surprisingly easy and gives a big boost to your credibility.

Maybe you offer customer service training courses for restaurant waitstaff. Writing an article that includes "Six Simple Things Waiters Can Do to Increase Diner Satisfaction . . . While Increasing Their Tips" can be a wonderful attention-getting tool. By all means, send it out by e-mail and in envelopes.

But wait, there's an even better way. Contact *Restaurant News* and offer to let it publish your article. Trade publications are always eager to get fresh content, so you should have no trouble at all getting your article placed. This also gives you the opportunity to include a byline that lets readers know how to reach you.

You've probably never even heard of *Restaurant News,* but I can assure you that it exists and is absolutely bulging with articles of interest to restaurant owners. I'm not unrealistic enough to suggest that many owners actually *read* these articles; they have restaurants to run. All of a sudden, even though very few people may actually read your article, you've become a published author. That's a real credibility enhancer. It also allows you to refer to yourself on the phone as someone who's been published in *Restaurant News.* For individuals who *do* read the article, they may even contact you before you pursue them. Wouldn't that be nice!

Whatever impact your article may have had on a potential customer, the result will be magnified if you simply mail out a high-quality photocopy of the article as part of your direct marketing efforts. Be sure to get the publisher's permission to reproduce the page on which your article appears. You can probably also acquire inexpensive tear sheets of the page from the publisher or even a large supply of the whole issue in which your article appears.

Don't worry that the article isn't inspired or perfect. Don't fret that few people will actually read it when it initially appears. In fact, don't even be concerned if nobody reads it . . . ever! Your goal is simply to warm up your prospects. The fact that your ideas and article have appeared in industry publications establishes your credibility in two very important minds: your prospects' and your own.

It's certainly beneficial to have prospects think of you as someone whose ideas are so important that they've been published in their industry's various trade magazines. It may be even more important, though, that you elevate your own opinion of yourself. Most of us consistently underestimate the benefits that we can provide to our customers. When your ideas are of sufficient interest to be published, this helps you to realize that your expertise is valuable. You speak a little more confidently. You carry yourself with an enhanced air of authority. After all, you've been published in *Restaurant News*!

USE E-MAIL (NOT SPAM!) TO BUILD FAMILIARITY BEFORE YOU CALL

Although snail mailing a series of articles or pamphlets continues to be a great way to get attention, there's a faster and less expensive way to achieve the same goal: make use of the tool already available to you in your e-mail software program. Many programs allow you to write and preschedule a series of communications you want your prospects to receive. Just as you might consider sending three successive letters with articles or pamphlets before placing an initial phone call, you can easily schedule a series of e-mails to accomplish the same thing. This won't even require your personal intervention to execute the process. A "sequential auto responder" feature does the work for you. Write a series, or sequence, of messages and determine how far apart they should be sent. Because e-mail software programs are evolving so rapidly, check your current version for instructions on how to accomplish sequential mailings.

Be sure that these e-mail messages don't appear to be form letters. Plug in prospect information wherever possible and customize your messages based on what you know about the prospects' needs. Your own in-box may be your best technique test lab. As you scan your own incoming e-mail, notice which messages you immediately dismiss and then make sure that your marketing messages don't look like those!

On receiving a prospect's first reply, abort the automated process and intervene manually or with a specialized follow-up system. You'll do more harm than good if your prospect inquires about one product line but then receives an automated message about something entirely different.

E-zines and Newsletters Offer Repetition and Value

Although electronic newsletters are no longer novel and you've no doubt noticed that your own in-box is clogged with unwanted e-zines and newsletters, these tools still offer you a tremendous marketing advantage. Authoring and distributing a regular periodic electronic newsletter is very inexpensive and offers you the chance to demonstrate your value to prospects again and again. Your name or your company name keeps showing up in their in-box. That builds name familiarity and paves the way for your subsequent calls.

Prospects probably open only a couple of issues before determining once and for all whether you'll earn their full attention. Make sure that what you send is brief and easily read. Dispense with all those fancy graphics. Deliver valuable content right up front. Make it worth your prospects' time to open and read the newsletter.

It's very important that your distribution be based on an "opt-in" system. When you initially let prospects know that you're willing to send them valuable information on a regular basis, be sure they want it! Do this by requiring they signal their interest by responding to your subscription invitation or specifically requesting the newsletter. If you don't, here's the big danger: With the advent of cooperative spam-blocking utilities, someone who receives your newsletter without having requested it may, with a simple click, report you as a spammer. Once that happens, even people who have specifically requested your newsletter will stop receiving it.

The creation and distribution of electronic newsletters is both an art and a science, and the technology is constantly changing. This is such a fast-changing and specialized area that it's well worth your effort to study the subject well before you launch your own electronic newsletter or magazine.

RESEARCH YOUR PROSPECT ON THE INTERNET; DON'T BE A STRANGER

How did we ever get along before the Internet? This phenomenal research tool allows us to preheat our prospects by gleaning personal facts about an individual or getting a thorough company background.

I personally experienced the power of Internet research during the conception and creation of this book. The editor for the project was to be Michael Cunningham, about whom I knew nothing. My literary agent set up an introduction call so I might bounce my ideas off the editor. I knew that this first call would be crucial in catching his interest, and I knew I had to do something unusual to set myself apart from the other authors who would be considered for the project.

My first step was simply to enter this editor's name in my favorite Internet search engine and see what came up. One Web citation was from the same geographic area as the publisher's Chicago location, and I noticed a reference to this particular Michael Cunningham's involvement in a literary project, *Wabash Magazine*. Getting warmer!

Having never heard of *Wabash Magazine*, I dug a little deeper on the Web and discovered that it was a publication issued by Wabash College, with which I was also unfamiliar. More digging.

At the main home page for Wabash College: A Liberal Arts College for Men, I discovered a button that allowed me to hear the Old Wabash school song. I turned up my computer's speakers and whipped out a dictation tape recorder.

At the appointed time for my first telephone conversation with the man who would become my editor, the literary agent acted as intermediary and introduced me. Rather than the usual, mundane, "Oh it's so nice to meet you. . . ," I began by simply pressing the play button on my recorder. The first sound

Michael heard from my end of the line was a melodic rendition of his college fight song.

Was this a hokey move? Absolutely. Unusual? Yes. Relevant? Actually, yes.

As I had envisioned the project, one section of the book—this one—would explain how successful salespeople research their prospects prior to making contact. Michael Cunningham was certainly a prospect for me because I wanted to sell him on the idea of selecting me as the author for this book. I'm quite sure that I was the only potential author who began our first conversation by playing back his rather obscure college fight song. That set me apart and preheated my prospect.

Always remember that your key goal in the opening moments of any preheating call is to capture the other person's attention. Your prospects are absolutely swamped with solicitations and information. Setting your initial contact apart from the others so that you warrant some favorable consideration is a tough task. The Internet offers you an efficient and effective tool for accomplishing it.

Think of the time and energy you put into researching your prospects as investments with significant potential long-term payoffs. Maintaining a focus on the value of the relationships you seek to establish helps you realize a significant return on your investment, and sometimes it can be a huge one. The important thing is to think beyond the hassle of preparing for your call, which might well not be worth it if you're just thinking of a single transaction.

A friend of mine is an expert in a very specialized field of real estate investments and has established a market niche that deals with single-tenant properties used for assisted-living facilities. She does business with the owners of buildings used by Alzheimer's clinics, retirement homes, and so on. The actual owners of the properties may be individuals, family trusts, LLCs, or any of several other forms of ownership. My friend's goal in cold calling is to identify owners of such properties who may be willing to sell or trade them for other investments.

Step one is to find the properties. This agent's approach ranges from noticing a retirement community right in her own town to using a rented list of such properties to searching the Internet and accessing various association Web sites.

Step two is to find out who really owns the buildings. Again, the Internet is an invaluable tool because she has learned that her best resource is the county assessor's online tax records. Find out who pays the taxes, and you're probably going to find out who owns the property. Although the assessor's records provide an entity and an address, these may be simply a set of initials (L&C Holdings, for example) or the name of a limited partnership. You can then go online and check with the secretary of state's office to find out who the officers and principals are for the entity listed as the taxpayer. When the taxpayer is a real estate developer, my friend has learned through her experience that it's best to go straight to the top. "I always call the president directly. If that's not the person I should be speaking with, that certainly *is* the person who can tell me who I *should* be speaking with."

Step three, the actual preheating call, requires a lot less time than steps one and two. She may actually locate and speak with the owner of the building only to discover that the owner has no interest in selling or trading. But that's not the end of the line. She makes it a point to ask for referrals, as it's likely that owners of such properties know other real estate investors, some of whom may be interested in selling or trading right at that time.

In one such research effort, my friend took the first and second steps on the Internet and eventually tracked down the property owner. He was an attorney. No, he didn't want to sell. Having invested this much effort, though, she made sure that she asked for a referral, and—what do you know—the lawyer mentioned an acquaintance who also owned an assisted-living facility. As a result of asking for the referral, she ended up with a successful $2 million deal.

Was it worth the effort to go through the research steps, even though it merely led to an attorney who didn't want to sell? Absolutely yes. But that's only the short-run return on her investment. Because she has developed expertise in such a specialized field, it's quite likely that both parties will be future buyers and sellers of other properties used as assisted-living facilities.

OLD-FASHIONED CORRESPONDENCE PAVES THE WAY FOR YOUR CALL

I always find it interesting that the more high-tech and modern our sales tools become, the more unusual . . . and often effective . . . the tried-and-true old-fashioned methods become. Think of birthday card mailings, for example. Just about every sales book and seminar advocates sending personal birthday cards to your best prospects and customers. But do you send them?

On my last birthday, I received calls, cards, and greetings from friends and family members. But when it came to my business mail, there was exactly *one* birthday card. It came from Anne-g Litwak, the mortgage broker who arranged financing on my most recent home purchase. I've certainly dealt with plenty of sales professionals over the last few years, yet Anne-g was the only person to put into practice such an old-fashioned selling technique. Do you suppose she set herself apart? Will I turn to Anne-g next time I need financing? Will I recommend her to friends who are buying homes? You bet I will, and I already have.

So what about the very old-fashioned technique of sending out precall postcards? As more and more sales professionals turn to electronic communications, old-fashioned tools like postcards become less common and therefore get more attention. It's surprisingly inexpensive to order a large quantity of full-color postcards that promote your products or services, including a picture of yourself! These are easy to pop off in the mail and also help your prospect visualize . . . and thus personalize . . . you in advance of your call. Check out the services that will actually handle every aspect of postcard mailings for you. They'll create the design, e-mail you a PDF file for approval, input your mailing list, and then print and mail the cards without your ever touching them. (Refer to the online appendix at http://www.HeatUpYourColdCalls.com for resources.)

What you can do, starting NOW:

- Identify the perceived affinity group of which your prospect would be a member and build those membership criteria into your initial prospecting approach.
- Ask questions at the beginning of the call to immediately involve your prospect.
- Ask for permission to use membership lists of organizations to which your ideal prospects belong. Ask about revenue-sharing opportunities.
- If you're using membership lists with explicit permission, say so!
- Seek opportunities to speak publicly and benefit from the implication of your authority and expertise.
- Join your local Toastmasters group or National Speakers Association chapter to hone your speaking skills.
- Write a series of articles or pamphlets that will appeal to your prospects and enhance your credibility.
- Identify the periodicals that your prospects probably read and get your articles published in them.

(continued)

- Use the sequential auto responder function in your e-mailing program to inexpensively make multiple contacts before you call.
- Always use opt-in, permission-based subscription strategies when you distribute your e-zine.
- Invest the time to research your prospects on the Internet before making contact.
- Send birthday cards and precall postcards. Even though they are old-fashioned, they're increasingly effective at setting you apart from your competition.

4

THE CRUCIAL SKILL OF REFERRAL GATHERING

W*hat we'll cover in Chapter 4:*

- Why the consistent practice of gathering referrals benefits all three parties, not just you
- How to gather more and better referrals by using a simple three-step process
- Heightening your chances of success with any new prospect by positioning yourself on the very top rung in the relationship ladder: an explicitly named referral

Attend almost any sales seminar or read any book on sales techniques and you're sure to be reminded of the value of gathering referrals from your current customers. Yet when was the last time that someone from whom you buy asked *you* for referrals? Although the practice makes all kinds of sense and is easy to do, very few salespeople put the technique into practice.

Referred prospects are much more receptive to your prospecting approach and are much more likely to buy. They tend to become more valuable customers who place larger orders for a longer time. But these aren't the only benefits of referral gathering.

Asking for and following up on referred leads is another way of strengthening relationships with the referring customers and keeping them on your relationship conveyor belt longer.

I often recommend that clients adapt and adopt a very effective referral-gathering technique used by the company that insured my cars when I lived in California. This particular company accepted only customers whose driving records were unblemished and who drove cars with low accident rates. If you'd been cited for DUI or drove a Porsche, this company wouldn't insure you at any price. It catered to the lowest-risk population of drivers and offered premium rates that were always the least expensive available. For as long as I lived in California (the only state where the company was licensed), I was a steady customer. One day one of its salespeople called me and said:

> "Mr. Walther, you're exactly the kind of driver who makes it possible for us to keep our rates so low. Thank you. You should be very proud of your driving record. I see that you've had no moving violations and have never been involved in any kind of accident either. We want to keep on providing the lowest possible rates for you and other very safe drivers and I'd be happy to help any of your safe-driving friends. This will allow us to keep serving you well, too, by ensuring that we only cover people with the lowest risk of filing claims. That's what keeps our rates low for you. I'll be happy to call your recommended referrals directly myself. Among

your friends, who are the two or three very safest drivers you can think of who also drive low-risk vehicles?"

Because she put it that way, I was happy to provide a couple of referrals, and I also felt a closer partnership with my insurance company. You can use a similar approach to get the same positive results with your customers. Follow the three simple steps outlined below.

STEP ONE: TELL YOUR BEST CUSTOMERS WHY YOU'RE ASKING *THEM* FOR REFERRALS

Let's face it, you have some customers you wish would go away and quit buying from you. They're more trouble than they're worth, and they're unpleasant to deal with. Getting them to pay is like extracting impacted molars, and they're just no fun. Don't ever ask *them* for referrals, because their friends and associates will probably also be pains to deal with. Ask only your *best* customers if you want to get referrals who will be both pleasurable and profitable to deal with.

Now, if you're going to be selective and ask only your best customers for referrals, how are they to know you think they're the best? Tell them! Start right off by letting your good customers bask in the attention they deserve. Just as my California insurance agent congratulated me for my outstanding driving record, tell your customer why he or she is so valued by your company. I'm not talking about buttering customers up with false flattery. I mean sincerely telling your great customers why you like dealing with them:

"Mr. Wilson, I deal with quite a variety of customers in my work, and very, very few of them are as pleasant to deal with as you are. I appreciate having you as one of my best accounts. You're always open-minded when I make suggestions, you're prepared with all the details when you call in to place your orders, and you make sure that your bills are paid on time. As a company, we appreciate you, and I myself appreciate you most of all."

Of course your customer is in a positive frame of mind now and feels good about your relationship with good reason.

STEP TWO: POINT OUT HOW REFERRALS BENEFIT YOUR CUSTOMER

The auto insurance rep who had called me explained that my rates could be kept low only by finding additional very safe drivers to insure. What she didn't say, but what turned out to be true, is that my friends appreciated my referrals, and I also benefited through *their* appreciation. The company saved me a lot of money on my insurance premiums. When I referred friends and they saved a lot of money too, my friends were glad that I had referred them.

When you ask for referrals, be sure to explain to your customers why it will benefit them to help you.

STEP THREE: ASK FOR *SPECIFIC* REFERRALS

My insurance representative didn't call and say, "Hey, know anybody I can call to try and sell some insurance to?" Her question was very specific. She was looking for only "the two or three very safest drivers you can think of who also drive low-risk vehicles." Specific questions make it much easier for your current customer to think of exactly the right kind of referrals to offer you.

When prompting referrals from your customers, make it easy for them to cooperate by asking specific, clearly defined questions: "Among your colleagues, there are probably a few purchasing agents at other companies who you know are both enjoyable and really on top of things. I'd like to call them and offer to be of service. Who are the two or three people you'd recommend I get in touch with?"

Referral gathering is a very profitable and rewarding way to sell. The practice also benefits your existing relationships by strengthening the partnership bonds you want to nurture with your customers. The specific way you prompt referrals determines how successful you'll be at getting them.

Staying in touch with customers, including calling for referrals, pays off with stronger, more enduring relationships that are worth more to both of you now and over the long haul.

REACH FOR THE TOP RUNG

Your key task, before making any preheating call to a new prospect, is to discover (or create) a relationship with your prospect. If you can tell a prospect that a friend or colleague referred you, you can quickly get to the top of the relationship ladder I talked about in Chapter 3.

If you sell dry-cleaning equipment in New York City, start by figuring out just how high you can position yourself in the relationship hierarchy.

Bottom rung (cold):

"Hi, I sell chemical-reducing programs; can we get together?" (Forget it!)

Climb up a rung by creating a perceived affinity group:

"I specialize in helping reduce chemical use for small, independent Manhattan dry cleaners like you."

An actual affinity group gets you still higher:

"I'm calling you, as a member of the Manhattan Independent Cleaners Association, because I can help you reduce your need for chemicals, as I've done for so many other members."

Climb even higher with an implied referral:

"I help cleaners like Wu's on 33rd sharply reduce their chemical use. Let's see if I can do it for you too."

A named referral gets you to the top rung:

"Henry Wu over on 33rd is one of my happy customers, and he suggested I show you what I've done to reduce his chemical use."

The surest way to increase your return on investment when contacting prospects is to make better use of your preexisting relationship.

W *hat you can do, starting NOW:*

- Identify the criteria that describe your very best type of customer, the kind you wish you had a lot more of.
- Mount a referral-gathering campaign, starting selectively with just those "best" customers.
- Begin your referral-gathering calls by explaining to your best customers why they *are* your best customers.
- Figure out why it's in your customers' best interest to provide you with referrals. Then incorporate this benefit into your referral-gathering approach.
- Craft specific questions that will help your current customers identify exactly who they should be referring to you.

5

OPEN DOOR, INSERT FOOT

W *hat we'll cover in Chapter 5:*

- How you must establish an atmosphere of rapport before you can effectively exchange factual information
- Helping to build or blocking rapport by means of your vocal image, including your manner of speaking and the specific words and phrases you use
- How every phrase you use in every conversation helps to form the image you project to the listener
- How what you say and how you say it and your specific word choices also shape how you feel, think, and act
- Avoiding shooting yourself in the foot by being aware of the common phrases that undermine your positive image and eliminating them from your vocabulary

The prospects you call make very quick judgments about you based on your manner of speaking. Your word choice, tone of voice, speaking rate, accent, diction . . . all contribute to your vocal image. It can either help to open a prospect's door or slam it shut. How you talk determines whether you'll encounter a warm reception or be frozen out.

The first moments of the call are the most crucial. That's why we're focusing so much attention on preheating your prospect by establishing your name familiarity before the call and emphasizing your preexisting relationship. But even if you have that relationship spelled out and your name is familiar, communication gaffes can block your headway. This trust building is a difficult and complicated process. Some of the groundwork takes place before the call, but when it comes right down to it, your communication style has to immediately grab your prospect's attention to begin building trust and rapport.

PROJECT YOUR POSITIVE ATTITUDE IN EVERY CALL

You have facts and information to exchange, but first the doors of rapport have to open. Rapport can be loosely defined as a feeling of sameness. When we feel rapport with others, the channels are open; we're on the same wavelength; we feel we could become friends we trust. There are lots of direct and explicit techniques for developing rapport. They include the following:

- Using the other person's name during the conversation (in moderation)

- Mentioning mutual acquaintances by name or referring to mutual experiences or backgrounds
- Asking questions about the other person's viewpoint, which demonstrates that you're not self-centered but are interested in understanding the other guy's position
- Stating openly that your aims are the same, that you both share common goals, and that this conversation is an opportunity to achieve mutual satisfaction

Without rapport, we don't fully communicate; both parties are less likely to accomplish their objectives. Rapport plays a major role in creating a successful outcome for the call.

CHOOSE POSITIVE, POWERFUL, ACTIVE LANGUAGE

There are two great reasons to use positive language when establishing rapport: First, people understand what you have to say more readily when it's stated positively. Compare "I can get you those samples in two weeks" with "I can't get you those samples until two weeks from now."

The second, more powerful reason is that positive, active words and statements form exactly the kind of "gets things done" image that does help get things done. To be perceived as a person who has definite answers, knows where you're going, and has authority . . . speak that way! Cleanse your vocabulary. Purge such words and phrases as:

"I can't."

Negative! Sure, you can't schedule delivery of your customer's order until Friday. Say "I *can* schedule this delivery for Friday." The facts are exactly the same except that the statement is more readily understood, and you're seen as eager to help instead of obstruct.

"I'm really not too sure."

Of course you're sure. You're sure that you don't know for sure. Say "I don't have that information now. I'll be glad to get a definite answer and call you back with verification this afternoon."

"I'd hate to . . ."

Rather than taking the negative approach and saying you'd hate to give a wrong answer, put the shoe on your other foot: "I want to be sure you get an accurate answer." You're going to track down reliable information in either case. Do it positively!

"I was going to say . . ."

Have you ever heard someone say "I was gonna say, but I won't?" Of course not! We say what we were going to say anyway, so why not just say it? You sound as if you're unsure of your statement's validity and want to precede it with a qualifier. This devalues your thought and makes you appear wishy-washy and wimpish.

"When will that be ready?"

Taking a positive, active, assertive role means that you focus on what you need and then poll others, adjusting where necessary. Instead of asking "When will that new customer profile be ready?" say "I'd like to have that new customer profile by Wednesday morning."

"I would think . . ."

You would? If what? If you had a brain and used it? Don't use indefinite, conditional phrases. State confidently and affirmatively, "I believe . . ."

"May I ask your name?"

Meek, meek, meek! You don't need permission to ask another person's name, do you? "What is your name, please?"

"Can I interrupt you for a minute?"

You already have! First, if you feel confident reading the other person's mood, determine if this is a good time to raise your point. If it is and your point is valid, go! Or ask, "Jane, I know you're busy, so when may we talk briefly about the Hambly project?"

"Can I ask you a question?"

You already have! If the question is important enough to raise, you don't need permission to ask it. If there's doubt in your mind, save the question for later when it's your turn to clarify.

"I'll have to ask someone about that."

Who are you? *No one?* Rather than saying "I have no idea about that; I'll have to ask someone," say "My expertise is in A and your question concerns B. I'll be glad to contact our B specialist and get the answer for you."

"Hang on a minute while I get something to write with."

You shouldn't even answer the phone unless you've got pen and paper ready or are within reach of your computer keyboard. This phrase clearly says "I didn't have the minimal foresight needed to prepare for our conversation. My work space isn't orderly enough for me to reach out and find a pencil, so I'll waste a precious moment of your time while I rummage around looking for one."

"Can you spell your name for me?"

What an insult! Are you implying that your prospect may not yet have mastered the correct spelling of his or her own name? The direct answer to this literal question would be "Yes, I believe I can." Say precisely what you mean instead: "Please spell that for me."

"They just won't do it."

People are always talking about what others won't do. "Those salesmen just won't turn their expense reports in on time." Rather than making judgments and predicting the future, stick with the facts. "They haven't yet done it." Better yet, take responsibility: "I haven't yet invited the salesmen to cooperate."

"If I can find out . . ."

Project the expectation that you will be successful. Say instead: "When I verify that answer . . ."

YOUR THOUGHTS, WORDS, AND ACTIONS ARE CONNECTED

Most people would readily agree that we sound the way we feel. If you're feeling tired and depressed, you'll sound that way. What few people realize is that we don't just sound like we feel, we also think and feel the way we sound.

If you say "I'll try to call you sometime later. If we could chat some more, would that be okay?" are you really being as proactive as possible? Talk like that and it's clear that you don't really expect the conversation to take place. As a result, you act accordingly—and so will your prospects!

To ensure the conversation *does* take place, say "I will contact you later in the week and we'll talk further. Is 2:30 Thursday convenient, or would first thing Friday morning be better for you?"

Speak with the expectation of success and you propel yourself toward success.

BE CONCISE

Chatting with friends is one thing. Communicating useful information with customers and prospects in business is quite another. Boil it down! Get to the meat of your message and say it once. People who speak in long, convoluted sentences impress us as muddled thinkers. To be perceived as a sharp thinker, get to the point.

Yes, it's important to develop rapport with your prospect. You're making a good investment when you take just a few moments to build rapport. Most prospects, though, want to get on with business. When your intuition and your customer's tone of voice let you know that you're in sync, get on with it!

SPEAKING POSITIVELY OPENS DOORS

Your aim is to create a warm and welcoming atmosphere so that your prospect will be willing to open up and discuss his or her needs. Then you can get busy and start solving them. Your manner of speaking and your word choice in particular are crucial components in helping your prospect decide you'll be worth talking to.

The language changes I recommend in this chapter are simple *but* not easy. (Yes, I'm intentionally using the word *but* because *simple* and *easy* are quite different.) Continually improving your ability to engage sales prospects in dialogue so they ultimately trust you enough to buy from you is an ongoing process. One of the most important steps you can take is to identify and then purge from your vocabulary those phrases that undermine your effectiveness. Be sure to visit http://www.HeatUpYourColdCalls.com for more resources that will assist you in this process.

THIRTEEN WORDS AND PHRASES YOU SHOULD NEVER SAY IN ANY CALL

Each day, every day, colleagues throughout your office, including your sales assistants and front-desk staff who have direct interactions with your customers, are unwittingly shooting themselves in the feet. They're using powerless expressions that interfere with your desire to project the positive, customer-friendly, can-do attitude that you want to get across with every customer contact.

In fact, chances are that *you* say many of these same things yourself without even realizing it. There's nothing wrong with the words themselves; they're probably being spoken correctly.

It's just that the impact they have on the listener is a far cry from how you want people to perceive you and your organization.

We've already touched on some recommended phrase substitutions. Now I'll identify 13 common offenders: words and phrases that you and your sales colleagues may be using with customers all day long without realizing the effect they're having.

1. "I'll have to . . ."

There's nothing at all unusual about hearing yourself say "I'll have to check the appointment calendar . . ." or "I'll have to check with someone about that . . ." or "I'll have to make sure that we can do that." The trouble with this phrasing is that it indicates to the customer that taking the action is a burden rather than a pleasure. "I'll have to" translates to "I don't really *want* to help you, but if I must, I guess I will."

We want all our customers in every interaction to come away with the feeling that we are truly pleased to be of service. So why use phrasing that suggests serving them is a burden? This phrasing example is perhaps the most pervasive and the simplest to change of them all. Any time you or a member of your sales team is about to say "I'll have to . . . ," replace that phrasing with "I'll be glad to . . ." or "I'll be happy to . . ." or "I'd like to. . . ."

It's easy to hear the contrast yourself. Notice the difference in the impression you get when you hear a colleague say "I'll be happy to check my appointment schedule" compared with "I'll have to check my appointment schedule." If you were the customer, would you feel better about hearing someone say "I'll have to get the sales manager to check for you" or "I'll be glad to get the sales manager to check for you?"

2. "I'll try to . . ."

It's so common to say things like "I'll try to get back to you right after lunch." The trouble is, every time you use the word *try*, you're telegraphing to the listener . . . and to yourself . . . that this isn't a firm commitment, and follow-through should not necessarily be expected.

If something's out of the question, you probably know that already. You and the person you're talking with are both better off if you avoid wishy-washy, hedging words. If it can't be done, say so now, during the call.

Make definitive statements about what you *will* do. This helps to project a definitive "gets things done" image for your colleagues and for your entire office. It also assists staff members in actually following through. They hear themselves making a commitment and realize they are now accountable.

3. "That's a problem."

When the customer hears you say "We have a problem with your order . . . ," or "Scheduling a demo for you next week is going to be a real problem . . . ," what is the impression that you convey? "Bad news ahead . . . this is going to be difficult . . . here's a situation I wish I could avoid. . . ."

Here's what you can say instead: "Scheduling your demo next week may be a challenge, and I'll do my best for you." There's a huge psychological difference between the terms *problem* and *challenge*. We seek to flee from problems; nobody wants more problems in life. Challenges, though, are a different matter. Challenges give us the opportunity to unleash our creative resources to come up with solutions. We look forward to the inner satisfaction that comes from having dealt with them.

Replace *problem* with *challenge* and you'll get more positive results.

4. "I'm only just a . . ."

In many sales organizations, the bulk of the cold calling responsibility falls on the shoulders of sales assistants. More complicated sales scenarios and technical questions may ultimately be handled by an account executive. If, in the course of prospecting for new customers, a sales assistant encounters a question that's outside his or her area of expertise, the wrong reply would be: "Well, I'm *only* a sales assistant, so I'm afraid I really wouldn't be able to answer that question. I'd have to get one of our account executives to call you back." The assistant would be much better off to simply say: "That's an excellent question, and I want to be absolutely sure that you get the technically accurate answer. I'll be glad to do the research and call you back with definite, reliable information. May I reach you between 2:00 and 2:30?"

People want to buy from individuals who are confident and sure of themselves. Be certain that you don't undermine your own credibility by making self-denigrating statements. Although it may be true that you've recently completed your company's sales training course and don't yet have years of experience, why say so? It makes you look insecure and undermines your credibility.

5. "I got lucky."

Very few of the triumphs you experience in your office may be fully attributable to good fortune outside your control. Positive outcomes almost always result primarily from good decisions, excellent judgment, and skillful action that you and your colleagues have undertaken. The advantage of giving yourself credit when things go right is that you help yourself recognize the factors that led to the positive outcome. Then you can replicate those steps when facing similar situations in the future.

I'm not talking about boastful egotism here. When you succeed in a challenging sales scenario, don't go beating your chest and proclaiming that you're the greatest salesperson ever. It is important, though, that you have this dialogue with yourself: "Wow, that was a great call! I achieved all of my objectives. What did I specifically do that created this positive outcome? I want to be sure I keep doing it."

Don't give dumb luck credit for the successes you and your staff bring about in your office. Each time things go right, ask yourself, what did I do to create this success so that I can do it again?

6. "I failed."

Obviously, things aren't always going to go right. You don't succeed with all, or even most, sales efforts. You won't penetrate every screen and you won't warm up every prospect. When you blow an opportunity, it's tempting to view the situation as a failure.

In life, as in sales, the individuals who experience the greatest long-term success are those who make the most mistakes. Although that sounds odd at first, the reality is that high achievers experiment, take risks, embrace new challenges, and seek to continually learn more and improve. Salespeople who experience far less success back away when they encounter setbacks. Rather than learning the lessons inherent in such "failures," they decide not to take any more risks. They get stuck. Worse yet, when things don't go right in the future, they seek to cover up and hide their perceived shortcomings.

Replace the phrase "I failed" with "I learned." Whenever things don't go exactly right, look for the lessons that can be learned from the situation so such things occur less often in the future. I've always liked what Henry Ford had to say about setbacks: "Failure is the opportunity to begin again, more intelligently."

Rather than saying "I've called six times and still haven't reached this guy. I'm failing!" say instead: "I'm learning that simply calling and calling and calling isn't a reliable way to reach my prospects. I'm going to sharpen my calling techniques. (And carefully study Chapter 6!)"

7. "If only I had . . ."

Winners in sales and life and winning members of your sales team keep their sights firmly focused on the future and what they can do to make it better. When there's a setback or a "failure," they get busy figuring out what lessons they can learn. Losers look back with regret and self-derision and beat themselves up about mistakes they may have made.

The trouble with focusing on the past is that there's not a darn thing you can do to change it. Fixating on what you may have done wrong previously keeps you stuck in the past. It's certainly helpful to do a postevent analysis to determine where crucial decisions or actions went astray or which sales strategies didn't work. The only way to move forward and avoid such situations in the future is to focus on what you intend to do now as you move ahead.

Replace "If only I had . . ." with "Starting now, I will . . ."

8. "Customers make me so upset when . . ."

The people who experience the greatest success in life and make the best salespeople are those who accept personal responsibility rather than blaming others when things don't go the way they'd like. Instead of saying "Those prospects make me so upset when they don't complete their applications before our meeting," focus on saying "I feel frustrated when I encounter prospects who haven't completed their applications before our meeting. What steps can I take to improve the situation?"

9. "But . . ."

Suppose you sit down to have an annual review with your sales manager and you hear, "Darlene, you've had a very good first year here, but . . . ," you know that you're immediately going to be on guard and prepared to hear some form of criticism or other bad news. It's only natural because the word *but* is perceived as an opposition or contradiction word. We use it when we want to put ideas in opposition to each other. "She's excellent on the phone, *but* her sales follow-through is rather sloppy."

One of the negative effects of using the word *but* is that it creates conflict between ideas and also between people. If your sales manager says to you, "You're very good at developing rapport with your prospects, but you just don't make enough calls," you get the idea that you're really falling short. If that same sales manager were to say, "Your ability to develop rapport is very good *and* you can be making more calls," you're much more likely to be receptive to his helpful feedback and increase your calling activity.

You can detect a subtle downturn in enthusiasm just about every time you use the word *but.* Strive to consistently substitute *and,* and you'll find that you generate more cooperation among customers and others, while at the same time opening your own receptivity to ideas.

Rather than saying to your customer, "Yes, you can reduce the per-incident costs of tech support services, but you'd have to sign an annual contract," replace it with, "Yes, you can reduce the cost of your tech support *and* have price protection with an annual contract."

10. "Is everything satisfactory?"

Does this sound familiar? You're dining with a companion at a restaurant that you feel is overpriced and overhyped. You both agree that the service has been slow, and you're not impressed with the quality of the food, not to mention the server's attitude. As you finish your meal, the waiter tosses out a perfunctory, "Is everything satisfactory?" Most of the time, most of us say, "Yes, it was fine." Why don't we tell the truth? The answer is simple: We can tell that the server didn't really want to hear the truth because of the way the question was phrased. Think how much more willing you would be to offer constructive feedback if the server had said, "We're always looking for ways to improve our service. What's one thing we should be working a little harder on?"

I urge you to make regular direct phone contact with at least a sampling of your customers, as well as with prospects who didn't buy from you. Make the calls personally to get firsthand feedback. Whenever you make those calls, be sure to do away with the typical, "Is everything going okay?" query. Instead, use the approach that's going to get much more valuable input: "We're always looking for ways to improve the way we serve our customers. Would you tell me two or three things you've noticed we could be doing better?"

11. "I disagree."

The trouble with the word *disagree* is that it somehow magically transforms itself somewhere between your mouth and the listener's brain. Although you didn't really say "You're wrong and my opinion has much more validity than yours," that's what the other person "hears." As soon as you say to the other person "I disagree with you," you're setting yourself up for conflict.

When you're talking with a potential customer about the wisdom of investing in your products or services or talking with a colleague about one of the office policies, resist the urge to utter the word *disagree*. It's sure to create conflict. You're much better off to replace it with "I *understand* what you're saying, and at the same time. . . ."

12. "Do you understand? Do you have any questions?"

There are two reasons why this form of question will not get you very far. Presumably, you're asking it because you want to be sure that you and the customer or colleague have a clear understanding between yourselves. This question, though, only gives you the other person's *opinion* of whether he or she understands. To be a superb communicator, it's necessary to take some extra steps.

First, be aware that this form of a question may well put the listener on the defensive. To embrace the notion of personal responsibility, you're much better off to say, "I want to be sure I explained that clearly." In other words, focus on finding out whether you did a good job of making something clear rather than on determining whether the listener is intellectually capable of grasping your meaning. This is another instance of a seemingly harmless everyday expression that we all tend to use without thinking how it can have unintended consequences. You say, "Don't you understand?" The other person may *hear* "He thinks I'm stupid and can't keep up with him, so now he's putting me to some sort of test to see if I can follow him." Of course that's not what you meant. Yet it may well be what the other person thinks you intended. So, prevent this possibility by clearly phrasing your question in a way that shows you are personally responsible: "I want to be sure I said what I meant. What did you hear?"

Second, you're best off to avoid all yes/no questions. Rather than asking *if* your customer or staff member has questions, ask "What questions do you have?" If there are none, it's easy for your listener to say so. This form of question makes it much easier for the listener to reveal what is not exactly crystal clear so that you can clarify further.

13. "To tell you the truth."

Just what is that supposed to mean? Do you usually *not* tell the truth? This is just one example of the many habitual phrases that raise questions about your integrity: "To be perfectly honest . . . ," "Frankly . . . ," "Let me level with you. . . ."

What these phrases have in common is that they signal to the listener that you do not behave with 100 percent integrity. If you did, it would not be necessary to alert your listener to the fact that you're about to parcel out a rare morsel of truth.

There is no substitute phrase I recommend for "To tell you the truth." Rather, I recommend an action: Live the truth! Your company's and your own reputation are founded on the principle of dealing openly and honestly with all prospects and customers. There is absolutely no substitute for conducting your business with the highest level of personal integrity.

This list of 13 no-no phrases is certainly not the exhaustive list of expressions that will get in your way. The point is, there are many. Truly mastering a positive vocabulary does not mean simply eliminating these 13 examples from your daily dialogues. This is a continual process, and you should always be self-monitoring your communication style. Let your colleagues and friends know that you want to consciously and constantly improve your vocal image and seek their help in pointing out your slips.

W*hat you can do, starting NOW:*

- Consciously seek to develop rapport with prospects by using their name (in moderation) and pointing out your common ground.
- Always choose positive phrasing: say what you *can do* rather than what you *can't do.*
- Ask friends and colleagues to help you monitor and become aware of negative phrasing in your daily dialogues.
- Get to the point. Once you've established rapport with your prospect, cut the chitchat and get down to business.
- For starters, purge the 13 powerless expressions from your vocabulary and use their more powerful, positive replacements.

READY, SET, DIAL!

Among the wide range of technological resources at your disposal, your telephone is still your most important tool. Even though lots of changes are certainly happening in the phone industry, from Internet-based VoIP communication technology to automated call-handling systems, your *personal phone technique* remains your most powerful tool for gaining your prospect's attention.

Why do we prepare thoroughly for face-to-face sales calls and other meetings but expect to "wing it" on the phone? The fact that we spend lots of time preparing for meetings and almost no time preparing for phone calls is especially curious, because we do so much more preheating and selling on the phone than in face-to-face situations.

You need a good road map . . . a sound strategy . . . to reach your desired destination. A "perfect call" proceeds predictably and logically through five distinct phases. In this section, we'll move through them to reach our destination: success!

6

TRANSFORM THE TELEPHONE INTO YOUR MOST POTENT PROSPECTING TOOL

W hat we'll cover in Chapter 6:

- Planning for successful outcomes by organizing your thoughts and writing out your objectives before each call
- Putting an end to the frustrating and time-wasting game of telephone tag
- Using your time far more efficiently by scheduling telephone appointments
- How to take advantage of the powerful benefits offered by sales automation software
- Turning automated voice mail systems to your advantage by building a messaging sequence that establishes your credibility
- Tapping the switchboard operator or receptionist as your information resource
- Rearranging your work area to minimize distractions and create an optimal prospecting environment

Your phone can be a major source of frustration. You and I have both sometimes slammed down our receivers, feeling more than a little annoyed at how difficult it can be to establish meaningful dialogue with strangers. Your telephone can also be your most profitable sales tool but only if you use it effectively. You prepare for in-person visits by planning your objectives and thinking about what you want to accomplish before the meeting gets underway. You should do the same thing with phone contacts. Get your ducks in a row before placing any calls. You'll be far more likely to achieve your objectives.

One of the best time investments for honing your phone skills is to use a Call Planning and Objectives Form. (See page 69.) For a downloadable form that you're welcome to print for your own personal use, please visit http://www.HeatUpYourColdCalls .com. The form helps you to organize your thoughts, gives you a place to jot down planning notes, and keeps you focused on the primary objective of your call. The key ingredients are the specific objectives you seek to achieve during a given call. These may be fairly loose, such as: "Let the customer know I am thinking of him, while raising his interest about our new line coming in the fall." Or you may set more definite goals: "Schedule an appointment for our first in-person meeting during my Detroit trip next month and discover the prospect's key buying motivations."

Heighten the odds of achieving some level of success by listing secondary objectives, and even a bottom line fallback objective. Resolve that, even if you aren't successful in achieving your first or second objective, you will at least make headway toward your long-range goals.

If you aren't using contact management software, as recommended later in this chapter, then the back of the Call Planning and Objectives Form is the place to record notes as you

CALL PLANNING AND OBJECTIVES FORM

CALL PLANNER

Caller: _____

Calling: _____

Number: _____

Time Zone: _____

	DATE	TIME
First Call	_____	_____
Scheduled 1st Callback	_____	_____
Actual 1st Callback	_____	_____
Scheduled 2nd Callback	_____	_____
Actual 2nd Callback	_____	_____

Estimated Time Needed _____ Minutes

Actual Length of Call: _____ Minutes

ACHIEVED?
Yes   No

First Objective: _____   ❏   ❏

Second Objective: _____   ❏   ❏

Third Objective: _____   ❏   ❏

Bare Minimum: _____   ❏   ❏

Key Questions to Ask: _____   ❏   ❏

Follow-Up Action: _____   ❏   ❏

talk. This means you'll want to hang on to the paperwork for reference during future conversations, and that's part of the reason contact management software is so helpful. Keep your focus on the objectives you're out to achieve and ensure that the call keeps moving in the right direction.

TELEPHONE TAG—YOUR PROSPECTS ALSO HATE THE GAME

Phone tag is a game known to—and despised by—all in business. But you don't have to play it if you apply basic discipline.

Reduce Frustration: Schedule Your Calls and Callbacks

Just as you schedule other key tasks throughout the day, allocate time for your phone calls. Get in the habit of reserving specific hours each day for placing the outbound calls you initiate and for fielding the callback responses you expect from others.

One of the most effective methods for short-circuiting phone tag is to make telephone appointments. I suggest a preliminary call, whether from yourself or from your secretary or sales assistant to your contact's secretary. Schedule a specific time just as if it were an in-person appointment. Then, when you reach the part of your day blocked for phoning, you will have appointments prescheduled. Packets of background information and research about your prospect and your call will be in order, and you simply check off the calls as you achieve your objectives. You and your assistant should both get out of the habit of scheduling indefinite callbacks. Go beyond "Have him call me when he gets back." Instead: "I'll call John again this afternoon. Is 2:30 a convenient time for him, or shall we make it at 4:00? Which time fits John's schedule better?" Loose requests merely support and perpetuate the frustrating game.

You can do the same thing when scheduling the other person's return call to you. You're always better off making calls in the proactive mode when you're doing the calling, but sometimes you must take the reactive position and handle a call on the other guy's turf. Rather than saying "Have him call me," be more specific: "I've reserved from three to four o'clock this afternoon for callbacks. What time in that hour is most convenient for John? I'll be expecting his call so we won't get stuck playing phone tag."

I always prefer to be the caller instead of the callee. We accomplish more faster when I have my agenda and notes in front of me and am mentally prepared to pursue specific objectives. Sometimes I have to be the callee in order to end phone tag, but I'll address important calls only when they have been scheduled in advance. That way, my secretary is alerted to expect the call, and we're able to dive right into the business at hand.

Let's suppose that your company's sales vice president is considering engaging me to deliver the keynote presentation at your upcoming annual sales conference. Naturally, there are several serious considerations necessary for my program to be successful. I'll need to know the overall meeting theme, your current competitive challenges, what sales training you and your colleagues have experienced in the last year, and exactly what your vice president's objectives are for the session. Those are serious considerations, and we're probably going to need a solid half hour to discuss them. Because I'll want to be certain that your vice president and I are both focused on this important call and free from distractions, I'm going to schedule the call just as if it were a face-to-face appointment. Doing so lets us both use our time more efficiently.

Although many of the sales calls you make will not involve quite so much detail, you're still always best off to invest the time to make sure that you and your prospect have each other's attention. One effective way to do that is to schedule the call and be the one who dials it.

I recently attended an industry trade show and handed one of the exhibitor's booth attendants my business card in exchange for a little leather notepad holder. I'm sure you've been at plenty of trade show booths where you've done something similar. Three weeks later, my assistant received a call from one of this exhibitor's salespeople. He said, "Please have George call me back when he gets a chance. We met at the ACCE trade show."

Although I didn't recall the individual, I did phone back, hoping that his cold call might serve as an example for this book. It sure did!

"Hello John, this is George Walther returning your call."

"Oh yes, George (stall/fumble), how was your name spelled?" (Sound of shuffling and typing as he attempted to locate his record of the call.)

"Was that last week?"

"No, you called today, about two hours ago."

(Sounding confused.) "Oh, ah, yes, I must have been calling because we met at the ACCE show."

"Well, I did attend the show, but I'm sorry I don't recall meeting you. Would you please refresh my memory?"

"Oh, I was at the booth wearing the red shirt." (Like I'm supposed to remember his wardrobe?)

By this time, just a few seconds into the call, it was clear that he was simply phoning from a long list of people who had exchanged their card for the leather notepad. He had no idea who I was and had attempted to deceive my assistant by making it sound as if we had enjoyed some extended conversation. The truth is, I had never met the guy. I just handed over my card because I wanted that free leather notepad holder!

Of course his call was not successful. He would have vastly improved his chance of success if he had made an appointment to phone me back at a specific time. He could have had his contact information right there in front of him instead of fumbling around and making a bad impression.

Another method of ending phone tag, the "time bomb" technique, can terminate the game altogether: "Please let Chris know that we'll ship the order to the Euclid Avenue address on Thursday. If she'd prefer that we use a different shipping location, just give me a call by the end of the day. If not, it's all set to go out the day after tomorrow."

Naturally, you'll want to be sure that the time bomb technique is used only in situations where there's no significant downside risk of misunderstanding. It would be a *bad idea* to say "Unless you call back by the end of the day, I'll enter an order for 1,000 units."

Ask a "Now" Question to End Phone Tag Before It Begins

Wouldn't it be great if you could take significant strides toward eliminating one of your biggest headaches by uttering a single word? You can! And that single word is itself very simple: *now.*

My experience has shown that you can reduce and eliminate about one-third of all telephone tag games by simply asking a question that focuses on the word *now.* You reach an assistant or secretary who says, "She's not available; can I take a message?" Don't leave a message . . . yet. First ask that "now" question:

- "Is she in another part of the building where I may reach her *now?*"
- "Does she have a cell phone where I may reach her *now?*"
- "Is there someone who works with her on this project I may speak with *now?*"

Be careful not to appear pushy or overly aggressive. Maybe your contact has simply gone to the bathroom! Still, asking that "now" question will get you closer to the conversation most of the time.

Schedule Phone Appointments

There's just no way around it: first calls frequently will not get through. One frustrating and exhausting part of reaching prospects is the series of ongoing and typically unsuccessful repeat attempts. Get through seemingly impenetrable front lines by:

- Increasing the odds of getting through the first time
- Reducing the number of repeat attempts that are necessary by making each call more effective

To cut the number of repeat attempts, be sure that you always make an appointment to call rather than just trying again later. Suppose a secretary takes your call and tells you that the executive you want to reach is out of town all week. Respond like this: "Tim, will Elaine be back on Monday? She'll probably want a day to get caught up, so I'll be glad to call on Tuesday. Are mornings generally better, or is she less swamped in the afternoon? Fine, I'll call at 2:30, if that looks clear. Tim, will you please note on her calendar that I'll be calling? I'll ask the switchboard to put me through on Elaine's line at 2:30 next Tuesday."

I'm not suggesting that Elaine will be hovering by her phone at 2:29 waiting for your call. But you do stand a better chance of reaching her by setting the appointment. Even if you *don't* reach her then, you still create a determined, professional image by following through as scheduled.

The very first impressions you create go a long way toward forming others' long-term expectations about how you'll behave later. Even though you didn't actually speak with Elaine at 2:30, your message with her assistant or voice-mail system made it clear that you're the kind of individual who takes commitments seriously and follows through on them. That's the profile of someone with whom Elaine will want to do business. (More about an effective messaging sequence later in this chapter.)

TECHNOLOGY ACCELERATES YOUR EFFICIENCY AND EFFECTIVENESS

There are plenty of commonly available, inexpensive technological tools that will help you make quick, positive first impressions. They're simply tools, though. You have to make the decision and commitment to use them.

Contact Management Software Helps You Move Ahead

Although it's hard to believe, most salespeople are still not taking full advantage of the inexpensive and highly effective contact management software packages on the market. The best ones available change over time, so I encourage you to check out the latest offerings with your software vendor. Many programs can achieve the same sorts of results, but I recommend that you choose one that is off-the-shelf rather than having custom software designed for your organization.

If you work independently and can make your own software decisions, I suggest that you ask your colleagues what program they use—and then buy it! There's a tremendous benefit to having friends who already use the program you choose. Calling tech support is one thing, but being able to turn to a friend and ask a quick question or brainstorm ideas about how to set up your various customer fields and make full use of the program's reporting capabilities can be a huge benefit.

Most independent professional salespeople I know use a program named *ACT!*, the market leader as of this writing. Several competing programs offer similar capabilities, but *ACT!* has effectively positioned itself as the most widely used, and that carries with it the inherent benefit of having a large installed base of users so you have plenty of places to turn for help. It's quite likely that somebody in your industry has already customized this program for exactly the sales scenarios you face each day.

The benefits of contact management software are many and include the following:

- **Organized and scheduled prospecting and follow-up calls.** When you schedule a block of time to sit down and start dialing, you'll have your calls already queued up and can refer to your list so you know who comes next. You simply move forward as the contact management program serves up the prospect database one by one.

- **Automated dialing.** One of the handiest features that you can find in some programs is the capability of dialing the phone for you. You want to eliminate anything that interferes with your momentum when placing outbound calls. If you can have your computer automatically dial your prospect's phone number for you, you'll find that you can place many more calls and give yourself fewer excuses to interrupt your momentum. Computers dial more accurately than you do, too.

- **Clear and simple note-taking capabilities.** During conversations with your prospects, you can type out notes of what they're saying as you talk. (Use a quiet keyboard so prospects aren't distracted by the sound of your typing.) There's a tremendous value in being able to look over these notes right in your prospect's contact record before future conversations to help you recall exactly what you talked about the last time you were in touch.

- **Immediate and future follow-up activity scheduling.** Most programs make it very easy for you to quickly send off an e-mail message or create a custom or form letter with very little effort. If the prospect asks you to call again in ten days, you can readily schedule that activity exactly as the prospect has requested so nothing falls through the cracks.

• **Flexible reporting capabilities.** One of the greatest values of contact management software is that it allows you to determine which of your lead sources are actually producing the most successful sales opportunities.

Many of the natural human failings that undermine sales professionals' effectiveness are directly addressed by contact management programs. Failing to organize callbacks, failing to make careful notes during conversations, failing to analyze the results of your efforts, and even failing to quickly and accurately dial telephone numbers all reduce your efficiency and effectiveness. The greatest advantage of contact management software is that it allows you to correct many of these shortcomings all at once.

It's surprising that so many people (myself included) typically use only a small percentage of their programs' capabilities. Even with software that I've used for years, each time I review the training manual I discover new ways to streamline the prospecting and selling process. If you're going to make use of a very powerful tool like sales automation software, it will prove to be a very worthwhile investment of your time to fully understand and exploit the program's capabilities.

Boost Your Efficiency and Effectiveness with a Headset

Who wears a headset when making telephone calls? Receptionists. Operators. Customer service agents. And the most successful sales professionals! There's nothing demeaning about using a telephone headset and there are tremendous benefits for doing so. In fact, efficiency-minded innovators at all levels of business, and especially sales professionals, find that headsets allow them to accomplish more—more quickly and more comfortably.

Any sales professional who uses the phone intensively will benefit from using a headset. These devices do the following:

- Improve your efficiency by freeing your hands so you can type or jot notes and reach for records
- Reduce distracting background noises so that you can concentrate your full attention on the call
- Cut fatigue by improving your posture and allowing you to get up and get your blood pumping
- "Brighten" your voice by letting you gesticulate and move around freely
- Contribute to your personal safety by keeping both of your hands free to drive when you're using a cell phone on the road

I'm not suggesting that you harness yourself to your phone for the day. But during those periods when you've reserved blocks of time for a long series of callbacks, slip on a headset and you'll breeze ahead.

Inexpensive Gadgets That Enhance Your Phone Power

Communicating conscientiously by phone is hard work! You're intently focused on the calls, taking notes and listening between the lines, giving feedback. The last thing you want to do is hasten the physical drain by staying in one spot. Slouched in your chair and tethered with a short phone cord, you can't help but sound somewhat sluggish.

To sound animated and lively, move around. Get your blood coursing. Be invigorated. Replace your standard short handset cord with a very long one. Unfettered, you can stand up and flex, fish out files, reach for a calculator, and so on. When you move about, you wake up your body, and thus your voice. Feel alert and you'll sound alert.

For the best benefits, combine headsets and long cords. You'll free up your communication style when you wear a telephone headset that has a very long cord or is cordless.

Now, you may think I'm nuts. But the fact is, I find it highly beneficial to keep an atomic clock beside my phone. Go buy yourself an atomic clock that is synchronized with the precise official United States time. It'll cost you about 20 bucks. It constantly receives radio signals from the official U.S. atomic clock in Colorado, and your display will show you the precise time. In my case, I consider it a matter of personal pride that if I say I'll phone you at 2:00, you can count on my calling at exactly 2:00. I begin dialing at 1:59 and actually hold off on entering the last digit until just a few seconds before 2:00. There's an extra air of confidence in your voice when you know that you're the kind of person who does precisely what you say you will do.

PENETRATING SCREENS

One of the most frustrating and time-wasting phone situations we encounter is confronting a confusing, disorganized, perhaps even hostile bureaucracy. Intentionally or not, the whole organization may seem bent on blocking your contact. It's not always the result of indifference, as with monopolistic utility companies or government agencies. Sometimes, even people who want to talk to us have built-in blocks that make contact nearly impossible. In the following sections, I offer advice on how to overcome these blocks.

Getting through a tangled bureaucracy or disorganized company, or tracking down an elusive prospect who probably assumes that your conversation won't be worthwhile, requires sound strategy. Success awaits those who play the strategy game rather than simply bashing themselves repeatedly against closed doors until they either collapse from frustration and exhaustion or break through. (It's rarely the latter!)

HOW TO CONVERT VOICE MAIL FROM FRUSTRATION TO FRIEND

The telephone technology that annoys sales professionals the most is their prospects' voice mail systems. (That goes both ways, too!) My audience members and newsletter subscribers consistently complain that when calling prospects, they leave message after message yet don't get callbacks. You can either be disgusted with voice mail systems and view them as completely frustrating hindrances or you can choose to view them as a technology tool that gives you an edge.

Face It: If They Won't Return Your Call, You Need a Different Approach

I know, I know. Your prospects *should* call you back. After all, you have been persistent and courteous in leaving them message after message. Smart and effective people recognize reality, accept it, and find a way to deal with it. The unfortunate reality is that most people you phone before you've established a relationship simply are not going to call you back. Deal with it!

The Messaging Sequence That Builds Your Credibility Before You Say a Word

Here's a very simple system for converting voice mail frustration into a selling advantage. Naturally, you'd prefer to make direct voice contact with your prospect rather than leave a voice mail message. However, if you're going to leave a message, do not—I repeat, *do not*—leave your name and number and ask prospects to call you back. They're not going to do it.

I recommend that you leave a very brief message indicating your preexisting relationship (refer back to Chapter 3) and explain that you'll call again at a specific time:

"Henry, my name is James Novak and I'm calling you because John Abrahmson has been using my landscaping services for his new home construction projects around Southlake. He told me that you also specialize in high-end spec homes and want them to look their very best before you put them on the market. The projects I've completed for John have contributed to rapid sales, and I'd like my landscaping to help you sell your homes as well. I will call you again tomorrow morning at 9:30 so we can talk about how I may help with your current projects."

I'm not unrealistic enough to suggest that Henry is going to be there to take your call at 9:30 the next morning. You're probably going to have to leave another message. This will be your second message:

"Henry, this is James Novak calling once again. I left a message yesterday letting you know that I'd call at 9:30 this morning, and its 9:30 right now. I fully understand that you're busy, so please don't feel bad about missing my call. Afternoons may be better for you, as they are for John Abrahmson, who recommended that I talk with you in the first place. I'll make it a point to phone you again at 4:30 this afternoon. If that won't be convenient, will you please have Charlene call me to schedule a better time? You may count on my calling punctually then. She can reach me at 555-1212. Otherwise, you may count on my call at 4:30 this afternoon."

So what's going to happen when Henry hears this message? First of all, he'll know right away that you're a person who follows through on your commitments. People make forward-projecting inferences in their judgments about others and are heavily influenced by what happens early in the relationship. So you're already taking steps to impress Henry that you're the kind of person who honors commitments. If you make phone calls on time, he'll begin to infer that you also complete landscape projects on time. Your message reminded him of your mutual connection to the referral source. You've also taken the extra step of making him *not* feel guilty about missing your prior call, which shows that you are courteous and considerate. You've shown that you respect his level of authority by recognizing that he's very busy and probably works closely with his assistant, Charlene. By the way, you know Charlene's name because you used the switchboard operator as an information resource. (I'll show you how to do this later in the chapter.)

You may well react to this suggestion by saying, "That's a lot of trouble to go to. Shouldn't I just be able to leave my number and have him call back?" Yes, you should. But he won't. Yes, it takes a lot of trouble to make contact with prospects. In this case, if you're in the landscaping business and you want to begin a new relationship with a high-end home builder that could endure for years with many profitable projects, isn't it worth the extra trouble you must go to in order to create that positive first impression?

Setting telephone appointments is one of the most powerful and simple techniques I can recommend for you. Doing so helps you organize your own time and shows your prospects that you're an organized person who means business. You follow through and do exactly what you said you would do, impressing your prospect with your level of responsibility and commitment.

THE OPERATOR OR RECEPTIONIST IS YOUR BEST INFORMED RESOURCE, SO USE IT

The starting point in any penetration strategy is the switchboard. In most organizations, unsolicited calls reach a switchboard or central operator, who normally does little more than connect you with the requested extension. Because few people actually regard this voice as a person rather than a human switching device, therein lies your opportunity.

Busy as they are, switchboard attendants have little human interaction on the phone. Many are actually lonely. And they can also be a fount of valuable information—if you tap them.

With the right approach, a well-phrased question, and some patience, you can converse with a switchboard operator. Regard her or him as an information resource and approach this knowledgeable person in a friendly, human way. Here's what you want to find out. "I know you're very busy with incoming calls, so put me on hold whenever you need to. Please tell me, who's the person most involved with purchasing janitorial supplies for your company?"

You want the practical, day-to-day reality, not just the organization chart. The switchboard operator is ideally situated to know who's really doing what. "Whom does she report to?" And if you *really* want to heighten your chance of reaching the intended party, call that person's boss first. Suppose you sell cleaning supplies and the person who can specify your product is Earl Lerner, the cleaning supervisor. If Earl reports to Hank Wynn, the facilities manager, call Hank first. You'll probably be referred back to the cleaning supervisor. But now, you are able to call and say, "I've been referred by Hank Wynn. Is Earl available, please?" You're in a much stronger position and far more likely to gain immediate attention. It's the old top-down approach salespeople have long used effectively.

Be sure to ask:

- **"How is his name pronounced?"** You should try to avoid any gaffe that you can. What worse way is there to begin a conversation than by mangling your contact's name? Get pronunciation cleared up with the operator before you reach your target's secretary.

- **"What is his secretary's name?"** Everybody loves to hear his or her own name, secretaries included. It's also helpful to sound as if you are already acquainted. "Hello, Janet? Janet, this is George Walther. Is Mort available, please?"
- **"Does she usually come in early or stay late?"** If you're attempting to connect with an elusive but influential businessperson, you can be pretty sure that she doesn't work nine-to-five hours. The operator may say, "Early or late? Why, Joanne must get here at sunrise." Now you know when to call. Whenever possible, phone at a time when your call won't be competing with dozens of other intrusions. You're also best off calling when the individual's secretary isn't guarding the gates. Calling before or after regular working hours will often get you right through to your intended contact.
- **"What's usually the best time to call that department?"** Simple question, valuable answer. Often, you'll get a response that not only helps you get through but also helps your intended contact get through the day. "Accounting? They're insane all day on Fridays and mornings are pretty hectic too. You're best off calling early in the week just after lunch."

Obviously, you won't always find a helpful switchboard operator. But even if you do only half the time, you're way ahead of the game. Most organizations have more than one operator, but even if there's only one, there's always a relief person working during lunch. Call again then.

We all unconsciously perpetuate phone tag by leaving messages like: "Just tell him I called," and "Have her call me back later." Your own secretary can effectively short-circuit endless phone-tag loops by consistently asking for and giving specific messages. The rule of thumb is simple: Never use vague terms like "call again later." Always cite a specific time and day when you'll be available to receive a call or when you'll call back.

STEP AHEAD WITH EVERY CONTACT

Whether it's leaving better messages or making sure that you arrange a specific callback time, the name of the game in ending phone tag is to achieve the objective of getting a step closer with each call. Very often, it will be necessary to make several calls before completing a connection. Rather than simply crossing your fingers and hoping, make sure that every call consciously takes you one step closer to the desired conversation.

CHANGE YOUR ENVIRONMENT TO IMPROVE YOUR PHONE POWER

Even the physical placement of the telephone on your desk influences what you're able to accomplish with it. In most offices, desk phones are placed right in the midst of the clutter. When that phone rings, it reaches out and grabs your attention. But as you speak, the papers you've just been working with, your stack of callback notes, and your spilling-over pile of priority projects are all sharing the same visual space with your phone. They distract your attention.

Be sure that your phone is placed so that you cannot see others in the office. Selling requires your total concentration. If you're facing a hallway, your passing colleagues will catch your attention and break your concentration. They'll also be tempted to enter your office to drop something off or to scrawl a note. Make yourself appear uninviting and/or inaccessible when you're on the phone.

Top telephone sales professionals, people whose daily earnings depend on their ability to persuade others, have long known that mirrors contribute to monetary earnings. It's true. People like to do business with those who sound friendly. To increase your chances of making headway with others on the phone, project a friendly tone of voice. The best way to *sound* friendly is to *look* friendly! No doubt about it. The shape of your mouth does influence how you sound. If you look sullen, you'll sound sullen. Smile and you'll sound friendly. Place a small mirror near your phone as a reminder.

Somewhere very close to the phone, keep a rapid-access file of the people who are most likely to call you. You take giant steps toward balancing the scale of control when you have available background material in front of you during a call.

By all means, keep a clock in plain view. Be conscious of the time you are investing in the call. When the value received doesn't compare favorably with the time you're spending, wrap it up.

Maintain this phone station as your sanctuary. Regardless of what happens to the rest of your office, keep this one small place neat and ready for concentrated action.

What you can do, starting NOW:

* Use the Call Planning and Objectives Form, and write out your specific goals before pursuing important prospecting opportunities.
* Replace vague "I'll call back later" messages with specific callback appointments.
* When your prospect isn't available, resist simply leaving a message. Instead, first ask a "now" question.
* Train yourself to fully exploit the benefits of your contact management software.
* Use a comfortable cordless headset or, when using a handset, fit it with a very long cord that lets you move around as you talk.
* Invest $20 in an atomic clock and ensure that you honor your commitments by calling precisely on time.
* Gather information from switchboard operators and receptionists to pave the way for your call.
* Rearrange your work area so that you're free from distractions and can focus on your calls.

7

PHASE ONE—YOUR
TELEPHONIC HANDSHAKE

What we'll cover in Chapter 7:

- Building the opening moments of your call around your strongest relation-ship statement to heighten your chances of making your call welcome
- Using benefit statements to immediately capture your prospect's attention
- How to transition from the handshake to Phase Two by using an open-ended question

If you can't get your foot in the door and make initial contact, you're sunk. Regardless of how smart, charming, and persuasive you may be on the phone, you've got to *reach* a prospect before anything can happen. That's why we've invested so much time and attention on leaving effective voice mail messages and demonstrating your reliability even before the conversation takes place.

Your actions before the call shape your prospect's perception of you. If you've called previously and left a message saying that you will phone again at 3:00, you start with a strike against you if you don't dial until 3:15. By the same token, if your call comes in precisely at the time you promised, you have an edge in preestablishing your credibility.

HOW TO MAKE YOUR CALL WELCOME

Think back to Chapter 3 where we focused on the importance of identifying your preexisting relationship with your prospect. Even if you have had to create a perceived affinity group, emphasizing this relationship at the very beginning of the call is the single best way of making your call welcome. Forget the extended, phony, icebreaker small talk. Have you noticed that every time a stranger begins a conversation with you by saying, "Good afternoon Mr. Walther, how are you doing today?" you're immediately on guard? It sounds as if the salesperson is buttering you up and attempting to lull you into feeling comfortable. The fact is, we're all wary of outsiders who want to gobble up our precious time. The very first challenge is for you to demonstrate to your prospect that you're not an outsider or time-waster.

EMPHASIZE YOUR PREEXISTING RELATIONSHIP

If yours is the very strongest type of relationship and you have been referred by a friend or colleague of your prospect, say so right now.

"Hello, Mrs. Sweeney. I'm George Walther, and I've been working with Linda Burkart, who recommended that I talk with you. My design team has been helping her create the new corporate image over at Boren Boating, and she told me a little about your current efforts to upgrade your graphic look. Thanks for taking my call. Let's see if I can be of help to you."

Maybe you don't have a direct named referral and are going to use the implied approach.

"Hello, Mrs. Sweeney. I'm George Walther, and I've been working with Linda Burkart to communicate the new corporate image over at Boren Boating. She's been very happy with the customer feedback she's getting on the new logo that you've probably seen in Boren's recent advertising. I've been noticing your ads and would like to find out how I may help you to update your graphic image. Thanks for taking my call. Let's see how I can be of help to you."

Or perhaps you're going to use the perceived affinity group approach.

"Hello, Mrs. Sweeney. I'm George Walther, and I specialize in helping to update the corporate looks of small businesses like yours in the Lake Boren area. I focus on smaller companies that have limited advertising budgets yet want to project a very professional corporate image. Thanks for taking my call. Let's find out how I can be of help to you."

Whatever the preexisting relationship you may have with this prospect, it's critical that you spell it out right up front. Think of yourself as someone who's buzzing the intercom at the prospect's apartment building. You're not going to be let in unless you quickly demonstrate that you're not just another stranger.

DEFUSE YOUR NUMBER ONE ENEMY: LACK OF ATTENTION AND INTEREST

You want this prospect, who doesn't really know you, to give up some of her most valuable resource: time. You want her to show interest and give you her full attention. But why should she? Start with benefits.

"All of our clients in the local area have experienced a significant increase in business after working with us, sometimes in the 15 to 20 percent range and almost always at least 5 to 10 percent."

USE THE TAKEAWAY TECHNIQUE SO YOUR PROSPECT BEGS FOR MORE

Your time and other resources are every bit as valuable to you as they are to your prospects, right? You're not going to squander your sales attention on people who are unlikely to buy and begin a profitable relationship, right? You wouldn't want to take time with someone who won't benefit from your services. You're going to concentrate your attention on those prospects who stand to truly gain from what you do. You certainly don't (yet) know if there's even the potential for a good fit with this prospect, so say so!

"I'm not sure just how useful our design services would be to you. I'll be able to give you a clear picture of how much we can help you in less than five minutes. May I explore just three questions with you? Let's find out if it would be worth our while to schedule a brief personal meeting."

I know there are plenty of sales trainers out there who recommend that you schedule as many meetings as you possibly can. That's not my view. If you went out on every appointment, you'd certainly find that most of your prospects were probably not going to be qualified to work with you. That means that you'd be overlooking some of your very best prospects while you're out chasing after those you'll later discover are just not qualified. Let's short-circuit this waste of time by doing some qualifying on the phone. (You'll find specific examples of qualifying questions in Chapter 15.)

Don't let your prospects get the feeling that you're overly eager to meet with anybody at any time. Your time and expertise are valuable. Let prospects sense that you meet only if there's a likely good fit between what they need and how you can help. Increase the perceived value of your appointments by asking questions designed to determine if prospects' situations warrant a meeting. Ideally, you want them to hope they qualify.

(Pardon me for being selfish and focusing on not wasting *your* time. What about your prospects? Let's not waste *their* time either.)

It's important that this crucial first phase of a call concludes by shifting the ball from your court to your prospect's. Sales professionals tend to jabber. We're all so impressed with ourselves, with our companies, and with our products that it's tempting to run on about ourselves. That almost certainly means that the prospect will stop listening and start erecting mental barriers. So shift the focus to your prospect: "First, please tell me what kind of feedback you have been getting about your current advertising."

Transition from Phase One to Phase Two by asking an *open-ended question*. The reason for this is threefold:

1. Asking this type of question gets your prospect talking. Because most prospective customers are sick and tired of

hearing salespeople yak on and on about themselves, this is your opportunity to immediately set yourself apart and show that your focus is on your prospect's needs rather than on yourself and what you have to sell.

2. Beginning with an open-ended question also gives you the opportunity to assess your prospect's preferred style of communication. It's important to mirror this person's communication style to develop rapport and set the scene for achieving maximum results. You can't adjust your speaking style and vocabulary until you find out how your prospect prefers to communicate. Listening carefully to the way he or she answers your open-ended questions gives you great clues about which communication style will be most effective with this individual. You'll notice and be able to mirror tempo, vocabulary level, and so on.

3. The final benefit of beginning with an open-ended question is that it gives your prospect an opportunity to begin shaping what will turn out to be your most effective sales approach. If Mrs. Sweeney tells you that she gets very little feedback about her advertising, that statement opens the door for you to explain how your services can help to create advertising that gets noticed and talked about. If she tells you that she's getting lots of very positive feedback about the advertising, you'll know that your most fruitful focus may be on ensuring that her letterhead, business cards, and so on tie in with the successful advertising theme. She may tell you that a couple of people have mentioned that her logo looks small-time or out of date. Again, this gives you a strong signal about what direction is most likely to be effective.

What you can do, starting NOW:

- Determine your highest relationship position prior to your call and identify it in your opening minute.
- Use takeaway statements to further prequalify your prospect.
- Ask an open-ended question as you transition from the first to the second phase of the call.
- Adjust your communication style based on how your prospect answers.
- Note the first thing your prospect says when answering the open-ended question and anticipate how you'll use that to your benefit later in the call.

8

PHASE TWO— DISCOVERY AND CONSULTATION

W *hat we'll cover in Chapter 8:*

- The transition from getting your foot in the door to building rapport and discovering your prospect's needs
- Building a bridge from the initial open-ended question to the multiple-choice questions that help your prospect steer you toward his or her concerns
- Demonstrating that your product or service is a perfect fit (if it is) with your prospect's needs

---

Wouldn't it be wonderful if all you had to say was "I sell state-of-the-art security systems for commercial buildings like yours. Would you like to buy one?" Your prospect would say, "Why, yes! That's just what I need. Could you please come right over?"

OK, now let's get real.

Selling is a process and sometimes a very long one. Each step in that process contributes to a feeling of rapport that you're actively seeking to develop between yourself and your prospect. Your prospective customer must learn to trust your expertise and integrity and in doing so reveals his or her set of needs. When you understand the prospect's buying motivations, you have an opportunity to satisfy them. If you see a good fit, you are obliged to assist your prospective customer as thoroughly as possible.

So the second phase of the preheating call is what I call *"discovery and consultation,"* because it consists of a series of questions, each of which helps your prospect open up so you can discover a little bit more about his or her concerns. The more you know, the more you can help. Each question gives you an opportunity to present another benefit.

Let's suppose you sell long-term care insurance, as does Richard Herzog of Assuracare, based in Bainbridge Island, Washington. Richard's marketing process involves everything we're talking about in this book. First, he builds his name familiarity and establishes his credibility and expertise by sending prospective customers a series of eight automatic contacts before any call takes place. These consist of four automatic e-mails and four mailed postcards. He spells out the perceived affinity group that is his specialty. The process is fully automated and does not require Richard's personal attention.

Before Richard places his first call, the prospect has already been preheated. Richard opens with his *telephonic handshake,* making reference to the e-mails and postcards. Once the door is open, he quickly moves the ball into the prospect's court by using an open-ended transition question, such as "I'm sure that in addition to my e-mails and postcards, you've been hearing a lot about long-term care insurance in the media lately. Tell me, what has been catching your interest? What are your primary concerns when it comes to long-term health care?"

Now, Richard listens! (That's an underutilized skill for most salespeople!) That's how he discovers his prospect's hottest hot buttons. He lets the prospect have his or her say and in the process learns what this individual is most concerned about. His follow-up is a series of carefully crafted multiple-choice questions designed to help the prospect reveal his or her most pressing buying motivations. Richard responds based on how his prospect answers:

"Yes, Mr. Hunsaker, I'm not surprised that you mention high medical costs, because that's the number one concern for people our age who are starting to think about planning for our future health care needs. Is your concern about cost based more on your cash flow or are you in a situation where you have children and want to be sure that they inherit your estate without its having been decimated by astronomical health care costs?"

Richard invests a great deal of attention to crafting a specific kind of multiple-choice question. It's one with three possible answers. His prospect may focus on cash flow, on preserving an estate for inheritance purposes, or on . . . *both!* Remember, the purpose of the multiple-choice questions is to help the prospect steer you toward the benefits the prospect most likely cares about. The more benefits that are brought to the surface of the prospect's awareness, the more likely the prospect is to let you help with his or her concerns:

"You mention some general worries about high costs. Are you more concerned about protecting yourself from rising premiums or gaining a general peace of mind in knowing that your children's inheritance is safe and sound?"

Again, Richard listens! Naturally, he's taking careful notes because the "consultation" portion of this second phase in the preheating call involves Richard's responding to each of the prospect's concerns. Remember, we're out to build on a feeling of rapport. The prospect "hears" that you've been listening carefully and responding to his or her particular concerns rather than simply reciting a list of benefits that some corporate trainer has told you to spew out. You're moving forward in the process of developing trust:

> "When you talk with a specialist about a complicated subject like long-term care insurance, are you more interested in getting a thorough understanding or actually eliminating the hassles of filling out applications and going through the process of securing coverage?"

Having made careful notes about what he's discovered are his prospect's concerns, Richard is now prepared to consult and focus on his benefits related to each of those concerns:

> "Mr. Hunsaker, it's clear from what you're telling me that you're already well aware that protection from the rising costs of medical care is your top concern, and that's exactly what I can help you with. I fully understand your desire to protect your children's inheritance, and that's one of the main benefits of securing long-term care insurance. You mention that you're equally concerned with gaining peace of mind from knowing that your kids are protected, and you also want to ensure that your future premiums will not become astronomical. Once you're covered, your premiums will not increase from the day coverage begins. You're going to notice a significant sense of satisfaction. You'll know that you've taken care of things for your kids. You also made

reference to avoiding the hassle of deciphering the specifics of policies and actually going through the cumbersome process of filling out an application. Again, that's my area of special expertise. Most of my clients end up doing little more than signing the document that I've helped them to prepare. It's a very easy process, and you'll have an expert on your side."

With some prospects, Richard can effectively complete the transaction during his series of phone calls. Other prospects are absolutely insistent that they must have a face-to-face meeting before reaching a decision. When that's the case, Richard adjusts his approach. Rather than selling long-term care insurance, he's "selling" an appointment. In this type of sales scenario, the actual purchase transaction may take place during a face-to-face meeting. Richard's goal is to develop such a feeling of trust during the call that his prospect will recognize that the personal meeting will be an excellent investment of his time.

"Based on all that you've told me, Mr. Hunsaker, I do recommend that we schedule 45 minutes together later this week. I can prepare a quote for you based on your specific age, health situation, and all of the other relevant factors that you've identified. I can also point out some of the important technicalities that vary from policy to policy and make sure that you receive the comprehensive coverage you want. And if it's appropriate, I can help by actually completing the application with you so that you immediately start enjoying that peace of mind you're after, knowing that your children's inheritance is well protected. I can meet with you in the late afternoon on Wednesday or first thing Friday morning. Which would be more convenient for you?"

GET YOUR PROSPECTS INVOLVED . . . SO THEY REVEAL VALUABLE BUYING CLUES

Notice that the bridge between the first and second phases of the call is a specific type of question: open-ended. Prospects will very quickly glaze over if all you do is yak on and on at them about what *you* feel is important. The whole purpose for contacting your prospect is to find out what concerns will motivate him or her to move ahead with you.

SHUT UP AND LISTEN TO AVOID THE BIGGEST MISTAKE IN SELLING

Despite all the sales books and training videos out there in the marketplace, salespeople are still prone to shooting themselves in the feet by jabbering instead of listening. As you ask your questions, focus on what your prospect tells you. I know this sounds obvious and basic, but the reality is that most salespeople just don't listen well. This is one of the reasons I recommend that you always have a notepad with you. Some sales professionals prefer to open a word processor window on their computer screen so they can type along as their prospect speaks. Be sure that your keyboard is a quiet one and that you use a headset with a noise canceling microphone so that your prospect isn't distracted.

What *you can do, starting NOW:*

- Plan for success by crafting a series of multiple-choice questions geared to match your benefits with your prospect's concerns.
- Design your questions with three possible answers: A, B, or both.
- After discovering your prospect's profile of needs, provide consultation by showing how your benefits match each need.

9

PHASE THREE—
WELCOMING OBJECTIONS
AND CONVERTING THEM
TO POSITIVE MOMENTUM

W*hat we'll cover in Chapter 9:*

- Reshaping your thinking about objections so you interpret them as positive buying signals rather than obstacles or roadblocks
- Altering your mental interpretation of what your prospect is saying when you hear an objection
- Streamlining and simplifying your objection-handling approach and mastering two all-purpose responses
- Understanding why you want to hear more objections, not fewer, and knowing how to get them

Let's be realistic. Prospects don't often jump at the chance to immediately buy from you or meet with you. They have reservations and usually need more information before making those decisions.

IT ALL STARTS IN YOUR HEAD; WHY YOU WANT TO HEAR PROSPECTS' OBJECTIONS

I'll say this again and again. And again. What you say, what you think, and what you do are all inextricably interrelated. Starting in Chapter 1, I stressed the need to eliminate the concept of "cold call" from both your thinking and your vocabulary so that you're not on the defensive when you approach prospects.

The exact same principle applies when it comes to *overcoming objections*. When you think of your prospects' concerns and/or confusions as objections that must be overcome, you handicap yourself. Something that must be overcome is something that must be bad. If that's what's in your head, it will influence how you react when you hear your prospects express a concern or request for more information.

One of the most common terms in most sales manuals is *overcoming* objections. We're going to take a different approach. We're going to *welcome* objections. If you think of an objection as something that needs to be overcome, you put yourself in a defensive posture. You'd tend to interpret the prospect's objection as really meaning this: "Gotcha! I've found a flaw in your persuasive argument. There's a chink in your armor. I don't have to buy from you now that I have figured out what my objection will be!"

An involved and engaged prospect is one who gathers more information in order to make a decision. Learn to hear your prospect's objection as a positive request for more information.

The most common objection, of course, is that your price is too high. Most salespeople are trained to anticipate this objection and steel themselves to quickly respond so they can triumph by *overcoming* it. The trouble with this approach is that it sets you up for failure. Whenever you take up a battle position with your prospects, you're bound to lose.

When a prospect says, "Your price is too high," here is what we *imagine* is really going on in that prospect's head:

"I certainly don't want to make any decisions, buy anything, or make any changes. So I have to find some way to defeat this persuasive salesperson. I've got to find some way to throw him off course. I know! It's an indisputable fact that the price tag of his product is higher than the price of the product I've been buying. There's my out! Once I make this clear, he'll go away, and I won't have to buy anything."

We're much better off to change the way we think about this particular objection. Instead, imagine that the prospect is saying this:

"Hmm, I don't quite understand. Your price seems to be higher than the price I've been used to paying, and there may be a good reason for that. I just don't know what it is. Could you explain that and help me understand, please?"

In other words, an objection based on price or anything else is not cause for you to tense up and become defensive or combative. It's instead reason for you to think, "Oh good, we're making headway."

The way you've always reacted to objections in the past is perfectly natural. It's part and parcel of the "overcoming" way of thinking. I want to help you reshape your thinking so that the very first reaction you have when you begin hearing an objection is "Oh good" instead of "Oh no."

So firmly plant in your brain the notion that all objections are requests for more information. They're *good* signs. When your prospects want more information, it means you're making headway. The appropriate (and most productive) reaction is to be glad. In addition, your prospects will be able to hear that reaction in your voice and may relax their own battle stance.

FLUSH OUT UNSPOKEN CONCERNS

Because your aim is to form a partnership with your customer, doesn't it make sense to eliminate any confusion or obstacles, even though they may not be obvious or even stated? If the person you're contacting has reservations about the very first transaction, whether that's scheduling a face-to-face meeting or making a purchase, you *want* to know what's holding your prospect back.

ALL-PURPOSE TECHNIQUES THAT HANDLE NEARLY EVERY OBJECTION

Even though your *thinking* may be straightened out when it comes to welcoming objections, it's important to have some verbal tools at your immediate disposal. Some sales trainers have written entire books on the subject of *overcoming objections*. I'm all for simplicity, and I find two objection-welcoming techniques are classics and highly versatile. They'll serve you well with just about every objection. Become adept at using them, and you really don't need 29 more techniques.

The Versatile "Triple F" Lets You Reply without Delay

Oh no, not that very old-fashioned "Triple F" technique! Hey, the reason it's been around so long is because it's so versatile and useful. And it works! The three Fs stand for Feel, Felt, and Found. These three words help you structure your thinking and prepare you to quickly respond in an unrattled and cooperative way rather than feeling flustered and argumentative.

Suppose you sell supplies for office copiers, and your prospective customer has asked about pricing on your paper. Sure enough, your cost per ream is higher than he's accustomed to seeing when he prices cartons of paper at his local warehouse store. After all, for such a commodity item, why pay more? That's exactly what your prospect is wondering, so it's incumbent on you to anticipate the question and answer it.

Your prospect says:

"The price of your copier paper is just too high."

You say:

"I understand exactly how you *feel.* In fact, many of my best longtime customers originally *felt* just exactly as you do. What they've *found* is that the modest dollar savings they could achieve by buying their own paper at a warehouse store is very small compared with the value of their time. They also notice that the low-quality paper you find at discount outlets typically creates more frequent paper jams. I'm sure you've had situations when your whole workflow slowed to a halt while you or your assistant opened up your copier to pull out jammed paper and then took the time to figure out just how much of your document did or didn't get copied."

How "I Understand, and. . . ." Eliminates Competitive Showdowns

Here's another approach that employs the same psychology when dealing with your prospective customer. Always remember, if you get into a battle or conflict with your prospect, you're the one who will end up losing. That's why it's so important to *not* set out to prove the customer is wrong. Remember, throughout this book we're focusing on those slight little differences in communication style that cumulatively make a big difference in how you make your prospect feel. It would be a mistake to say, "I understand, *but* at the same time. . . ." *But* is a conflict word. In the previous example with copier paper, it would have the effect of saying this:

"I recognize that you have noticed the higher cost of our paper, *but* you're missing the important point of the total cost. You fool, don't you recognize that it's very costly for you to take time to go to the warehouse discount store? What about paper jams? Didn't you even stop to think about the high cost of interrupting your office workflow to clear the jams that are so common with cheap paper? You're completely wrong in thinking that our paper costs more. (You idiot.)"

It's possible that you may have an intellectual duel with your customer and come out the verbal victor! You may definitively prove that your customer is wrong. But you won't get the order.

Our whole orientation should be to *welcome* objections rather than seek to overcome them:

"I *understand* your concern about paper costs, and you're certainly correct that the price per ream is higher with our premium quality paper as compared with discount warehouse store brands. *And at the same time,* I know you're concerned about eliminating unnecessary, hidden additional costs. Although the cost of the discount off-brand paper itself may be lower, the inconsistent moisture content of those off-brands results in more frequent paper jams, which lead to huge hidden costs as your office workflow is disrupted. Of course, your time is valuable, so we need to consider *that* cost if you're running off to the warehouse store whenever you run out of paper. So even though our paper does cost more per ream as you've identified, it also saves you from unnecessary workflow interruptions. Our direct delivery, which is included, saves you the time and inconvenience of having to pick it up yourself."

Always Fish for More: "What Are Your Other Concerns?"

You want to get all the objections on the table and dealt with right now. Adopt the attitude that objections lead to sales because they are signs that the prospect is indeed interested and wants further information and clarification. This is not a battle, and you are not out to "win." Because you want to begin a partnership with your customer, it behooves you to flush out all the unspoken objections. But don't call them "objections." Doing so would only reinforce the notion that you are in conflict with your customer. So even though you think you've dealt with all possible objections, it's always worthwhile to add the "What are your other concerns?" question before moving on to Phase Four.

W *h a t   y o u   c a n   d o ,   s t a r t i n g   N O W :*

- Consciously replace "overcoming objections" with "welcoming objections" in your words and thoughts.
- List the several most common objections you hear, and adapt the "Triple F" and "I understand, and" approaches to handle them.
- Always flush out unspoken objections by asking for more.

10

PHASE FOUR— HELP YOUR PROSPECTS MAKE GOOD DECISIONS

What we'll cover in Chapter 10:

- How to fundamentally change your thinking about *closing sales* and focus instead on the value of opening profitable long-term relationships
- Gaining an understanding of *net present value* and understanding why it's worth investing your attention to get this valuable buying relationship started right
- Thinking of *asking for the sale* as a natural element in the logical process of helping your prospects do what's good for themselves

---

You'll often hear sales trainers urge you to "Go for the close!" In fact, they'll frequently emphasize the point by triumphantly punching a clenched fist in the air. But wait, we're not heading into battle! If scheduling a face-to-face appointment with you, or buying your product, or taking any step forward in a buying relationship would not be a good decision for *your prospects,* it won't work out well for *you* either. After you have flushed out, welcomed, and addressed all of your prospects' concerns, you'll have a very good idea of whether you have the makings for fruitful relationships. If you do, it's your responsibility to help your prospects make a good decision.

NEVER EVEN THINK, MUCH LESS SAY, "CLOSE THE SALE"

Once again, it's very important to eliminate certain ingrained sales terminology. The word *close* carries with it the notion of finality, yet what we're about to do is *initiate* a relationship, not end one. It's entirely inappropriate to talk about closing at this point. Always remember that your thoughts, words, and actions influence each other. If you *talk* about closing, you *think* that way. And when you *think* about finality and ending things, you *act* that way. It's likely that this kind of thinking and speaking will be subtly communicated to your prospects.

I've worked with plenty of sales professionals who, on consummating a sale or scheduling an appointment, hang up the phone, stand up, beam a smile, pound one fist into the palm of their other hand, and exclaim, "I closed him!" This is precisely the *wrong* reaction. It communicates finality when you're actually just getting started.

WHY OPENING RELATIONSHIPS PRODUCES VASTLY MORE PROFITABLE SALES RESULTS

Think back over the whole marketing strategy we've been talking about here. Producing maximum profits from customer relationships requires establishing, nurturing, and salvaging long-term relationships. Even if the particular sales scenario you're dealing with will likely yield only a single purchase activity, you still have the opportunity to create a relationship in which there are future referrals, upgrades, product improvement suggestions, and so on. Whether the ultimate outcome of your preheating call is to produce a sale or to schedule a subsequent appointment, think of this phone call as the start of a potentially profitable long-term relationship.

The Wisdom of Calculating Lifetime Values

Lifetime value is a concept that helps to keep the big profit picture in focus. The true value of a customer relationship is not the value of just a single purchase. In fact, you may even experience a direct loss from an initial transaction. Your organization's financial analysts can calculate the lifetime value of a customer relationship by answering a few questions. If you're successful at welcoming aboard a new customer, how long will that relationship be likely to persist if you consistently nurture it? How many transactions per year may you expect from this customer if you treat him or her right? What's the cumulative value of those future transactions? Analysts can then perform a rather complicated mathematical calculation to determine the *net present value* of the anticipated future revenue flow.

Let's return to the Chapter 6 example of an individual selling landscaping services to builders. It would be shortsighted of the landscaper to hope that he'll be able to close a $5,000 landscaping job. He should instead be thinking, "This small builder completes about eight spec homes per year. That's $40,000 worth of landscaping each year. This could potentially end up as a five- to ten-year relationship, so we're really talking about a quarter to a half-million dollars." (For simplicity's sake, we'll skip the financial calculation that would yield the net present value of the future revenue stream.)

Don't you think it would profoundly affect the way you handled the prospective landscaping job for a contractor if your goal were to *open* a half-million dollar relationship instead of to *close* a single $5,000 sale?

ALL GOOD SELLING BOILS DOWN TO ONE SIMPLE DECISION MODEL

I know exactly how your prospects decide whether they'll buy from you. It's the same way we all make decisions about most everything in life. And it's really simple.

Picture the person you wish to persuade standing in front of you, facing you, with each hand at about shoulder level, palms facing up. It's almost as if you're looking at a human scale or balance device. In fact, the most basic view of the decision model is that people act as though they're human scales. On one hand, they're considering how much they expect to *get* by taking the action you recommend. On the other hand, they're measuring how much they will have to *give up* to get it. If what they're going to *get* far outweighs what they have to *give up* to get it, they tip in the direction of yes. But if the price is very high, or the hassle factor is high, or there's no clear understanding that significant benefits will result from saying yes, your prospect says no.

Now imagine this prospect facing a television and watching a commercial touting the benefits of a snazzy new vegetable slicer kitchen device, instead of facing you. The announcer explains how you'll impress friends with your fancifully sliced salad ingredients. Then he tells you how you'll save money by purchasing potatoes and making your own french fries inexpensively and shows how you'll save time by preparing hors d'oeuvres in a flash. And you'll even reduce pain by experiencing no tears at all when you cut up onions! With each new benefit, the hand that's weighing out the "what will I get" side of the balance gets heavier and heavier.

At the same time, the announcer is also trying hard to eliminate any perceived weight on the "what do I have to give up to get it" hand. There's an unconditional guarantee. Shipping is included. Three easy payments and so on. While one hand's weighed down, the other's practically weightless.

The announcer wants you to decide that you'll pick up the phone and order a kitchen slicer. So he makes it a point to make the benefits side of the picture very heavy. He also lightens up the other hand to make sure you recognize that it's very easy to receive those benefits. If the "what do I get" is heavy enough and the "what do I have to give up to get it" is light enough, you can't help but tip in the direction of saying yes. If the benefits are missing or aren't heavy enough or if the time and money and hassle side of the picture is too great, you won't buy his slicer.

Now that you have a visual image of how prospects make their decisions, let's build a verbal framework that's highly versatile and applies to your preheating phone call as well as to your face-to-face appointment and subsequent sales calls. It also works whether you're selling the value of an appointment or persuading an established customer to order a new line of your products or make a change to his normal purchase activity.

The goal of your call is to help your prospect make a good decision . . . to tip in the direction of yes. Summarize and play back the benefits you've talked about, clarify that you've addressed the prospect's objections, and then recommend that your prospect take the action you're suggesting. (We'll revisit the value of using the word *recommend* in Chapter 13.)

Suppose you sell mobile corporate document-shredding services. You've begun your call by spelling out your relationship, whether that's based on creating a perceived affinity group or (it's hoped) using your named referral.

You've used open-ended and multiple-choice questions to discover your prospect's concerns, and you've offered consultation by matching the benefits of your service with what your prospect cares about. There have been objections you've welcomed and addressed. Now, it's time to help your prospect make a favorable decision.

"Ms. McQuaid, as we've been talking about your security concerns, it seems clear that your sensitive corporate information is vulnerable right now, and you're appropriately concerned about that. You've let me know about your uncertainty concerning our offsite solution, and I have explained that the actual shredding and destruction take place within our secure truck before we even leave your parking lot. As I've explained, the cost for service amounts to having a very inexpensive insurance policy for your company, and you'll actually be saving on the expense of purchasing your own shredding equipment. Your staff will be working more efficiently by not handling the shredding themselves. Based on all we've talked about, it seems very clear that this is a service you should begin immediately. What I *recommend* is we begin by having our implementation specialist deliver the secure containers to your office next Tuesday and then schedule the shredding truck to be at your facility on Friday just after lunch and again on each subsequent Friday. That means your documents will be destroyed before the weekend, and you'll have peace of mind knowing that each Friday afternoon you can leave the office confident that your security is assured. I think it's important for us to get this first shredding scheduled right away. All we need to formalize the service is your signature on the annual agreement. Would you prefer to receive that by fax or as an e-mail attachment?"

As you've logically moved through the preceding three phases of the call, you've helped the prospect to see why this decision makes good sense. Now, you make it easy for the prospect to say yes by recapping what you've covered, stressing the benefits, reminding your prospect about your responses to the objections, and recommending a simple action.

Sure, it's possible that new objections may surface at this point. You know what to do: First, be glad you're hearing these positive buying signals. Then be ready with your "Triple F" or "I understand, and . . ." techniques; stay on track, helping your prospect make the right decision.

W*hat you can do, starting NOW:*

- Whenever the term *closing sales* pops up in your thoughts or your vocabulary, replace it with *opening relationships*.
- Calculate the *net present value* of your typical successful customer relationship to help you recognize the value and importance of helping your prospect reach affirmative decisions.
- Practice incorporating the word *recommend* as you help your prospect decide.

11

PHASE FIVE—THE EXTRA STEP THAT SEALS THE DEAL (THAT FEW SALESPEOPLE EVER TAKE)

W *hat we'll cover in Chapter 11:*

* The importance of showing—rather than telling—new customers that they've made a good decision by buying from you
* Exhibiting superior follow-through and concluding every call on a positive note
* How the five phases of the effective call all flow together to create positive outcomes

Just as your prospects are highly influenced by what happens at the beginning and at the end of a relationship, they'll also be particularly attentive to what happens at the beginning and the end of your phone call. You know all about "buyer's remorse," and you want to be sure that it doesn't undermine your budding relationship with a new customer. So use the concluding phase of your preheating call to ensure that you've solidified your customer's belief that he or she has just made a good decision.

HELP YOUR PROSPECTS REALIZE THEY'VE MADE GREAT DECISIONS

I do *not* recommend that you say, "You just made a very good decision." This sounds like typical salesperson talk and almost immediately makes your prospects start thinking they've made a mistake. Rather than *saying* your prospects have made a good decision, *show* them with your follow-through.

THREE WAYS TO CONCLUDE EVERY CALL ON A POSITIVE NOTE

A truly effective preheating or sales call includes three finishing touches: confirmation, extra value, and appreciation.

What you say now, in the concluding moments, can demonstrate to your prospects that you are indeed a conscientious professional who follows through with accuracy. If you have scheduled a face-to-face follow-up appointment, now's the time to restate the details. Clarify any special instructions such as parking arrangements or suite location. If you've just taken an order from your customer, *recap and confirm* the details.

The *extra value* item is your opportunity to pass along any additional piece of information that will increase the value your customers will receive. If you offer a strong guarantee, remind your customers now. This can help to alleviate any potential postcall buyer's remorse. You may also want to include a surprise bonus to enhance the value. This is also a good time to ask for referrals. Most sales professionals wait until the buying relationship is well established before seeking them (and most of them don't even do it then!). Be sure to review Chapter 4 about asking for referrals. The attention you'll give to a referred prospect reflects favorably on the person you're asking. So why not do it now?

Finally, it's hard to overexpress your appreciation. Graciously conclude your calls by thanking your new customers. Instead of just saying "Thank you," seek to offer something more specific. Saying "Thank you for your business" is nice, but it's much nicer to single out a particular detail: "Thank you for being so clear with your driving directions; I appreciate your time and look forward to seeing you on Tuesday at 3:30 in your office."

TAKE ADVANTAGE OF YOUR ELECTRONIC "PARTNERS" TO FURTHER SOLIDIFY YOUR GAINS

One of the best ways to add that extra positive impression at the conclusion of a conversation is to confirm important details either by fax or e-mail. I've always been impressed by sales professionals who take that one extra little step by quickly sending a fax that confirms an order or appointment. Although e-mail is even faster, it's not necessarily better. You can often set yourself apart from others by employing older technology. Almost everybody sends e-mails now, but many of them are blocked by security filters. Sending a fax is perceived as almost old-fashioned these days; old-fashioned courtesies, however, can help set you apart from other salespeople.

PUTTING THE FIVE PHASES INTO ACTION

Let's review the five phases of a call with a complete example and see how they flow together. Suppose you periodically purchase supplies for your computer equipment from a catalog supplier with a wide range of software and hardware. You've recently heard about the benefits of voice-processing software and have purchased a voice recognition program. The software itself is bundled with a headset microphone to use for capturing your dictation. A couple of weeks after your purchase, you've noticed that the program is taking quite a while to "learn" the way you speak and is still making errors as you dictate.

Although you've routinely placed orders online in the past, nobody from the supply company has ever contacted you. You're about to receive your very first phone call from a sales rep there. Let's listen in and overhear how the salesperson proceeds through all five phases.

Jan, calling from PC Provisioner: "Good morning Mr. Walther, this is Jan calling from PC Provisioner. You've been ordering computer supplies from us for about two years now. Thank you! *(Introduction/Relationship)* I'm calling because I see that you normally order online every couple of months to get laser toner and inkjet supplies and occasionally some new hardware. I noticed that earlier this month you purchased a voice recognition program, and I may be able to help make it work a lot better for you. Let's find out if I can offer a suggestion or two that will enhance your experience with the program.

"Tell me, what has been your experience with the program so far?" *(Begin Discovery and Consultation with Open-Ended Question.)*

George: "Well, I'm actually very excited about how this software works. I understand that there's a learning curve involved, and I have to let the program get used to the way I dictate. It's been a little frustrating because in my business I use specialized terms that apparently are not in the program's main dictionary. That will just take some time, and I see that it's improving each time I use it. One thing that *does* slow me down a lot is that the program seems to miss little words. It will often leave out a 'the' or 'and' even though I'm positive I said the words clearly."

Jan: "Yes, I understand how frustrating that can be. I've had experience with voice recognition programs myself and have noticed the same thing. You'll definitely get better results if you're very careful about the positioning of the microphone. It should be right at the corner of your mouth, not in front of it. Your very best bet for improving recognition accuracy is to use a top-quality noise-canceling microphone. I see that when you ordered the program originally, it came bundled with a standard-quality USB microphone. You'll experience far better results with one of the top-end choices. We now carry a very comfortable Sennheiser microphone that will give you absolutely top-notch recognition. I do have them in stock, and they're priced at $150. Our users report that this is an extremely comfortable microphone. The mic element itself is large enough so you can easily position it at exactly the same spot each time you dictate. It's also earphone free, which increases your comfort as there's nothing pressing against the side of your head." *(Present Benefits)*

George: "One hundred and fifty bucks! I already suspected that the microphone included with the software package might not be the very best I could get, so I went to a local retail computer store to check out other mics. They range in price from $30 to $50. One hundred and fifty dollars for some fancy imported German microphone is outrageous!"

Jan: "I know just how you feel, because after all the Sennheiser is costing about three or four times the price of most other midquality microphones. Many of my customers who end up using the Sennheiser mic felt just the way you do about the price. What they've found is that the recognition accuracy is much higher than any mic they can buy at a local retail store. That means their dictation time is slashed dramatically. Just as important, their frustration levels have dropped because they hardly even need to edit what they've dictated. *(Feel/Felt/Found)*

"In addition to the price, what other concerns do you have?" *(Seek and Welcome More Objections)*

George: "Well, you said that it's headphone free, but I really like my headphones on the current USB headset-style microphone. I use the playback feature so that when I'm correcting

some text, I like it when the program plays back what I originally dictated and helps me remember what I meant to say."

Jan: "Yes, the playback feature is very helpful. With the Sennheiser, the same feature still works just great using your computer's speakers. It's also nice to be able to answer your telephone
without having to slip your headphones off. The mic stays right
in place, so as soon as you hear the phone ring, all you have to
do is say 'Go to Sleep,' and the program turns itself off. You can
go ahead and answer the phone, wrap up the conversation, and
then reactivate the program and resume dictating. *(Welcome
Objection/Focus on Benefits)*

"I recommend that you order this new Sennheiser mic and
experience the recognition improvements for yourself. There's
a real advantage to using it now while your program is still in
the early stages of its learning process. I have your account information here on file, and I can send that out today by Second
Day Air with no additional shipping charge." *(Recommend Decision, Add Urgency, and Relieve Risk)*

George: "Well, as long as it's guaranteed, I'll give it a try."

Jan: "Great, I'll make sure that ships out today. We'll use
your standard address on Coal Creek Parkway, right? As you
know, your mic is guaranteed for 30 days. Say, I noticed that the
HP toner cartridges that you normally order about every three
months weren't included on your last order. How many would
you like me to add to this shipment so you'll have them on hand?
Great, the two toner cartridges and the Sennheiser headset microphone will come in the same box, and you are scheduled for
a Thursday delivery. By the way, I'd like to thank you for having
been our customer for almost two years now. I certainly appreciate your willingness to give this new Sennheiser microphone
a try. I'll process this order and e-mail your confirmation right
now; thanks again." *(Confirm/Extra Value/Appreciation)*

I'm not a proponent of using verbatim scripts. I believe the
prospect will always be able to tell if you're simply rattling off
some rote script that's been prepared for you. Once you under-

stand the flow of a successful call and recognize the value of each phase in moving your prospect toward a position of a solid buying relationship with you, you'll make your points most persuasively when they're coming from your sincere beliefs.

What you can do, starting NOW:

- End each call with a recap and verification of important details. This shows your customer that you're extra careful.
- Seek opportunities to add an extra value right at the end of your call. This may take the form of an upgrade or cross-sale, or you may ask for a referral.
- Remind your customer of your guarantee to relieve any postcall remorse.
- Fax order details following the call to ensure that your communication is not blocked by security filters.

GET PAST THOSE HANG-UPS

Successful sales careers include plenty of setbacks along the way. (And probably a few hang-ups!) In this section, we'll salvage some of the common situations that may be getting you down—prospects who don't want to meet with you; sales approaches that just aren't working; prospects who flat-out won't buy; and systems that make you work too hard for too little results.

Often, you're not out to consummate an immediate sale. That might take place after a much longer sales cycle, such as when you're selling insurance or some big-ticket industrial equipment. In fact, the immediate outcome you seek may be to schedule a face-to-face appointment.

Quite often, your prospect seems unable to reach a decision, even though you carefully proceeded through the call phases detailed in Part Three. When that happens, you'll need to administer CPR.

Despite your very best efforts, some calls just don't produce the outcome you were really hoping for. That doesn't mean they're wasted, though. In this section, you'll see how even a "no sale" call can still yield tremendous benefits.

12

GETTING THE
APPOINTMENT

What we'll cover in Chapter 12:

* Applying the "human balance" sales model to the intangible transaction: convincing your prospect to meet with you
* Adding those extra benefits that help an indecisive prospect tip toward "yes"
* Relieving risks in your prospect's mind by directly addressing his or her greatest fear

If the purpose of your call is to schedule a face-to-face appointment with your prospect, visualize the prospect standing in front of you with palms turned up as in the decision model covered in Chapter 10. You must make it clear there will be significant benefits to taking time out and meeting with you. You've also got to show that such a meeting presents minimal inconvenience. That same decision model applies if you are selling a product or seeking to schedule an appointment: You must make the weighty benefits clear and make it easy to decide favorably.

STACK THE DECK BY BUILDING ON THE BENEFITS OF ACCEPTING YOUR OFFER

Keep the visual image of that decision model in mind as you're talking to your prospect. Because you want the prospect to end up tipping in the direction of a "yes," you must pile on the benefits side of the balance until it's very heavy.

Suppose you sell insurance and the next step in your sales sequence requires a face-to-face meeting. The purpose of your preheating call is to convince your prospect that meeting with you will be worth his or her time. You're not selling insurance in your phone call; you're selling the appointment. Remember, your prospect is standing there with both palms turned up, thinking, "As busy as I am, would it really be worth my time to meet with this person?"

"Mr. Root, based on what you've been telling me, I do recommend that we reserve a half hour to sit down together and review your situation. I'll be able to look at the provisions of your current policies and give you an analysis right on the spot. We'll see whether it makes sense for you to combine your various policies with a single carrier. I'll also be able to tell you about how much you could save by doing so. Or if your current policies are already perfect for you, I'll certainly tell you so. You'll come out of this appointment either knowing that you're already very well protected at a reasonable price, or you'll find out that you could be better pro- tected for a lower price. I suggest we plan for Thursday afternoon. How does your schedule look at 3:00?"

Is your prospect tipping in the direction of "yes"? Add more weight to that side of the balance:

> "While we're together, Mr. Root, I'll be glad to give you a handy insurance policy organizer binder. If you're like most people I help, you have several insurance policies—for your home and car and health—and they may not all be in one place. With this binder you'll be able to keep them well organized for immediate access when you need them."

LIGHTEN THE LOAD BY FOCUSING ON "WHAT DO I HAVE TO DO TO GET IT?"

To help your prospect tip in a favorable direction, you need to make one side very heavy and the other side very light. Eliminate any obstacles that may be preventing your prospect from saying yes. In the case of *a product sale,* prime "lightening" benefits include, but are not limited to, the ease of setting up an account, your strong guarantee, and the ready availability of your tech support personnel.

In the case of selling an *appointment,* your primary obstacle is prospects' imaginations. They visualize themselves in some uncomfortable appointment that goes on forever and from which they have trouble escaping. Although they may not say so, they're worried that you're going to gobble up their entire afternoon. So you heighten your chances of success by directly addressing what they aren't saying (but are imagining):

> "My initial review of your various policies should take no more than 20 minutes. If it looks as though you're well covered, I'll be able to tell you so and help you set up your policy organizer binder within a half hour. If I uncover some significant savings by combining policies

with a single carrier, I can get you rolling with an application, so you'll at least know how much you'd save. That will take no more than 45 minutes."

THE IMPORTANT ROLE OF SWEETENERS AND RISK RELIEVERS

What's that phrase you keep hearing on late-night television infomercials? "But wait! There's more!" Marketers keep adding a little bit extra to make your scale tip. Take a cue from them and do the same with your appointment-setting calls. Look for any extra benefit you can spell out that may just make the difference to help this prospect decide it will be worth meeting with you or making the purchase. I call these *sweeteners* because they sweeten the deal with just that little bit extra.

Most people imagine there's risk involved in doing business with someone new. What if they get stuck with a product or appointment that isn't as effective as the salesperson said it would be? What if the promised brief meeting ends up being uncomfortably long and it's difficult to get the salesperson to shut up?

Add in *risk relievers* to address these concerns. Tell your prospect that you'll have a timer with you at the meeting and when it hits 45 minutes, you'll stand up to leave unless the prospect asks you to remain longer.

Refer to the example of the takeaway technique in Chapter 7, which is another good way to let your prospect know you are no more interested in long appointments than he or she is.

USE DOUBLE VISION TO FOCUS ON SHORT- AND LONG-RUN GOALS

When you're contacting prospects with a specific sale in mind, it's relatively easy to have a single focus. Setting appointments, though, requires a different kind of vision. Yes, you need to keep your eye on the immediate goal of getting yourself in the door. It's also crucial that you keep the long-term view in mind.

Since 1902, 3M has been known around the world as a premier manufacturer and marketer of everything from waterproof sandpaper to Post-it® Notes and NASCAR racing caps. Gary Hult, 3M's ESPE professional relations manager, has been selling for 3M for the last 30 years. He's invested the last two-thirds of his career helping 3M Healthcare's 3M ESPE dental division build great relationships in the field of restorative dentistry. 3M ESPE manufactures and markets more than 2,000 products and services designed to help dental professionals worldwide, ranging from infection-preventing face masks to nearly miraculous bonding materials.

Gary's not specifically concerned with the sale of a single order of masks or adhesives. He takes a much longer-term view: he's selling relationships.

Top dental professionals often band together in local study clubs, where they exchange clinical procedure tips and practice management ideas with their dental colleagues and keep up-to-date on the latest dental treatment procedures, equipment, products, and business ideas. One of the most effective ways for 3M to build relationships with leading dentists is to schedule educational seminars at these clubs to demonstrate its commitment to enhancing dentists' successful dental treatment procedures. These seminars also provide an opportunity for stress-free exposure to 3M ESPE's latest innovative products when the participants are using them during the hands-on exercises pertaining to the treatment procedures.

For Gary, that means his short-term sale requires building rapport with the study club directors so they'll invite him to make a presentation to the members. This presents an interesting challenge, because the club directors who perform more specialized treatments on patients typically do not use 3M

ESPE's general restorative dentistry products in their own practices, even though individual club members do.

Even though salespeople are commonly counseled to go straight to the top and reach out to the president or other senior officer of their target company so that they'll eventually be referred down to an individual who can buy from them, Gary also works from the bottom up. To further his long-term goal of building a long-lasting relationship, he asks members about their needs and wants, so he can pass these along to the club's director.

When Gary reaches the study club director, he starts off by mentioning the names of the individual members he's spoken with and some of the background information he's obtained from them. Right off the bat, that demonstrates he has invested time and energy to find out about the needs of members (his ultimate long-term customers). He relates those concerns to the needs of the director (his immediate short-term customer). The director wants to ensure that his members are getting great value from club meetings, and Gary shows how involvement by, and collaboration with, 3M ESPE can make that a reality.

After decades of experience selling to general dentists, Gary has learned that it's sometimes in the company's best interests *not* to sell 3M's products. Because his primary focus is on building long-term relationships with his ultimate customers, the restorative dentists themselves, his conversations with them quite often reveal needs that 3M's product line won't directly address. In this case, he directs the dentists to other suppliers who offer just what they need. This demonstrates added value, which earns him credibility and trust and is crucial to his long-term goal of building great relationships, and ultimately benefits 3M ESPE.

When you're in the challenging position of calling to schedule a face-to-face appointment, always employ the short-focus strategies that will get you in the door, while never losing sight of the big picture and working toward building long-term, trust-based relationships.

What you can do, starting NOW:

- Employ the *human scale* model so that you visualize your prospects standing before you. Do what you must to make them tip toward "yes."
- Focus on the specific benefits your prospects will realize from the appointment itself, not from the eventual sale.
- Relieve prospects' imagined risk by realistically stating how long an appointment will last while restating its benefits. Be very specific and avoid such unbelievable phrases as "This should only take a few minutes."
- Maintain a dual focus. Yes, you want to schedule an appointment. You also want to make progress in fostering a long-term relationship.
- Consider starting at the bottom in an organization to research the benefits that will most likely appeal to your ultimate prospect.

13

REVITALIZE YOUR SALES WITH "CPR"

What we'll cover in Chapter 13:

- Understanding that when customers aren't buying, your most productive course of action is to reexamine how you're selling
- Realizing that the features of your product or service are of little consequence to customers because they care only about benefits
- Getting long-term buying relationships started right by using the Consult-Personalize-Recommend model

In Chapter 10, we talked about how to help your prospects make good decisions in the context of the five phases of your effective preheating call. There is no single skill more crucial to your success in sales than your ability to be persuasive. Suppose your prospects don't follow your lead and take the action that you're convinced is in their best interest. (Unfortunately, that's not too hard to imagine.) It's easy to dismiss the situation by saying that the prospects just didn't want to go along with you.

The ultimate truth of your personal responsibility forms the most important foundation for my philosophies about selling. In that special (and far too common) situation when you're absolutely convinced that your prospect should be buying from you but isn't, your most productive remedy is to realign your thinking (and your language) about the selling process. Remember, I'm certainly not suggesting that you can sell anything to anybody at any time. I am, though, positive that the very best viewpoint for you to adopt is that when customers aren't buying, it's because you haven't used the approach that will work with them most effectively.

It's all too easy, once you're on the phone talking to a prospect, to slip back into old habits and start gabbing about yourself, your product, and your company. Do what's best for your customer by shaping your sales strategy into a very simple model I call *CPR selling*.

PUTTING THE CONSULT-PERSONALIZE-RECOMMEND SYSTEM INTO PRACTICE

When you're not experiencing the sales results you want, ask yourself this question: Are my thoughts, words, and actions all aligned toward the goal of bringing prospects to life? Your aim is not just to set an appointment or consummate a sale. The purpose of preheating your prospect is to begin a relationship, so CPR is an acronym that serves as a very appropriate analogy. Although we're not talking about cardiopulmonary resuscitation, we certainly are talking about vitalizing a buying relationship.

Notice that I say "buying" rather than "selling." Successful salespeople are those whose customers *want to* buy from them, not those who force a sale. Follow this simple three-step process:

1. **Consult.** Begin with an open-ended question or two that gets your prospects to open up and tell you about their needs, primary concerns, and communication style. Follow it up with strategically crafted multiple-choice questions.
2. **Personalize.** Match your prospects' needs with your benefits *if* there's a good fit. If there isn't, find another way to help them and move on to serve prospects who are better qualified to enter a long-term relationship with you.
3. **Recommend.** Provide counsel about the solution that you believe will best serve your prospects' interests. Use the word *recommend* to remind yourself of your consulting role and to show your prospects that you're thinking of their best interests.

Let's put the CPR selling system into practice with an example: One of my sales training projects involved an outbound program marketing custom-calling features for customers of a leading phone company. The company was offering call forwarding, call waiting, and speed dialing. The salespeople weren't having good luck when they called residents and attempted to explain the features. For example, they'd phone someone in a suburban area and essentially say:

> "We're offering subscribers in your area call waiting and call forwarding. This means that if you're on the phone and someone else tries to reach you, you hear a tone in your ear, and you can switch to the second call. Call forwarding means that you can designate a number anywhere in the world where you'd like your calls forwarded, and they'll automatically be switched to that number. Would you like to sign up?"

Would *you?* Who wants to hear a tone in his ear? Very few people are interested in being able to shunt their calls to someone else's phone. The salespeople were talking about features.

Nobody's interested in features. Customers are only interested in the *benefits* they'll receive.

C: Consult. The starting point is to ask questions. As I pointed out in the five phases of the call in Part Three, asking good questions gets your prospects involved, shows that you're focused on them rather than on yourself, and yields important clues about the benefits that are most likely to be of interest to a particular prospect.

The starting point in restructuring the phone company's outbound sales program was coming up with questions that would help reveal customers' needs that the features could satisfy:

> "Mr. Nudelman, when people say they have a hard time reaching you, do they usually say your line's often busy or that you're never around to answer the phone? When you're away for the weekend or working long hours, are you more concerned about the danger of burglaries at your home, or are you worried about missing important calls?"

The starting point in effective selling is to find out about your prospect's needs—not what you have to offer but what your customer needs. If Mr. Nudelman says that people can't ever reach him because he's always on the phone and that rising crime in his neighborhood is a concern, we know something about what his needs are and what benefits may appeal to him.

P: Personalize. The next step, after consulting to find out what the customer's needs are, is to personalize the benefits you offer to meet the expressed needs:

> "Mr. Nudelman, I know what you mean about crime being a concern. My neighborhood's been getting worse too. One benefit of the call forwarding feature is that you

can always answer your home phone even when you're not at home, the way I do. Studies show that burglars often call before they break in. When there's no answer, they think the coast is clear. Many of my customers forward calls to their cell phone. That way, even if a burglar suspects you're not at home, he hears your voice when he calls to check and you've prevented a problem.

"You also mentioned that people complain about busy signals and have trouble reaching you because you're on the phone a lot. The thing heavy phone users like you most appreciate about call waiting is that callers can always reach them, even while they're talking to somebody else. Rather than reaching a busy signal, they reach you. You can switch back and forth between the two calls easily and either take a message or call one party back later. It's very convenient."

R: Recommend. The key to succeeding in sales is meeting prospects' needs. *Consulting* lets you find out what they are. *Personalizing* lets you show prospects how they will personally benefit by having their needs met. Rather than forcing a sale, truly effective salespeople make sure they're in a position to *recommend* that prospects take advantage of solutions to their needs:

"Mr. Nudelman, based on what you've told me about your concerns for security and the problem of people not being able to get through on your line, I *recommend* that you take advantage of both of these new services. You can save 15 percent on the monthly charges by ordering both at once. Of course, the call forwarding will also help you cut down on missed calls when you're working late or away for the weekend. Would you like me to expedite these services for you or just have them added at the start of next month?"

Sales professionals should always adopt the goal of meeting as many customer needs as possible. Doing so creates short-term and long-term customer satisfaction and profits.

CONSULTING TO DISCOVER NEEDS

Asking questions, or *consulting*, is the first and most important step in developing any buying relationship. When I'm called on to help organizations train their people to sell more effectively, managers often ask, "Can you help us with some sales scripting? We want our newer people to know what they should say." I decline. To start selling relationships off on the right foot, representatives shouldn't be *saying*. They should be *asking*.

All sales encounters should begin with questions designed to do three things:

1. Show prospective customers that your focus is on them and their needs, not on yourself and what you're selling.
2. Gain immediate insights about your prospects' preferred style of communication so that you can tune in and match it.
3. Uncover your prospects' most immediate concerns.

There are three varieties of sales questions: open, multiple-choice, and yes/no. Let's cover the least useful variety first. If you're asking any question to which the answer may be yes or no, change your question. These monosyllabic answers just don't give you much information to work with, and you don't get your prospects truly involved in a dialogue.

A multiple-choice question is much more useful than the yes or no type. If you're helping a customer decide which motor home would be best, ask: "Do you plan to take a lot of short weekend trips, a few longer journeys during the year, or perhaps both?"

Multiple-choice questions give your prospects an easy way to help steer you toward the benefits of the greatest interest to them. Still, they're not the very best place to begin, because the answers tend to be short, giving you little information about a person's preferred style of communication. Moreover, you don't really know which multiple-choice questions are most appropriate until you understand your prospect's needs a lot more thoroughly.

Start with open-ended questions. The motor home salesperson would ask: "Tell me a little about the kind of traveling you want to do with your motor home."

Listening attentively to the answers gives you valuable insights about a prospect's most important concerns and shows you the style of communication that's most likely to be effective with this person. Your actions show that your primary interest is in your prospect's needs rather than in your own particular inventory of products or services.

If, after asking good questions and carefully clarifying a prospect's answers, you detect a good fit with what you offer, you're ready to move ahead. If not, say so. If the products and services you offer aren't likely to be a good match for a particular prospect's needs, it's best to refer the sale to an associate or offer to be of help in some other way. This is also a good time to ask for referrals.

HOW TO PERSONALIZE YOUR BENEFITS

If you do find a good fit, though, you're ready to *personalize*, the *P* in CPR. Match your prospect's answers to your benefits so you can demonstrate their alignment.

This is in stark contrast to the approach many salespeople take. You may have just completed a new product training session and know that your product offers 11 outstanding benefits to customers. Some salespeople feel that they must explain every one of those wonderful benefits. It's almost as if they're saying, "Don't interrupt me! I just memorized all 11 benefits, and I've only gotten through 3 of them so far. Shut up so I can tell you about the others!"

Benefits are not universally beneficial. Each prospect has a different profile of needs. That's why you took the time to *consult* at the beginning of the call. The *P* component should flow naturally, based on what your prospect has told you she or he cares about most. Sure, you can deliver 11 fabulous benefits. But if this prospect's answers to your questions indicate that 3 of them are of particular interest, focus on those 3. By asking good questions, you'll know which benefits will be most persuasive in moving this prospect toward a purchase decision.

THE MAGIC OF RECOMMENDING WHAT'S BEST FOR YOUR PROSPECT

Now, put the consultative selling philosophy into practice and make specific recommendations for your customer. The *R* of CPR is the step that leads to results in sales: *recommending.*

It's important that you literally use the word *recommend.* The continuing theme of thoughts being connected to words being connected to actions applies here as it does throughout the book.

Make it your single-minded goal to offer your prospective customers a sound recommendation. You can't do that unless you know what's best for each of them. You can't know what's best unless you start by asking good questions. In other words, if your ultimate goal is to earn the right to use the word *recommend,* you'll naturally take the appropriate steps to get there.

Later, in Chapter 16, I talk about how you can consistently improve your selling effectiveness. I'll urge you to randomly analyze at least one call every day. Ask yourself exactly what words came out of your mouth just before the prospect decided to either accept or reject your suggestions. I assure you that using the word *recommend* is your most reliable approach to gaining acceptance.

The initial sale is the beginning, not the end, of the relationship. Always seek to maximize the total lifetime value of a buying relationship by starting it off on the right foot and concentrating on using the CPR approach. Your aim must be to bring a prospect's needs to the surface so that you can meet them. Never hesitate to terminate your selling effort with a prospect if there just isn't a good fit. Remember, selling something to somebody who isn't likely to be happy over the long haul exposes you to many costly risks, including negative word-of-mouth publicity in the marketplace, a tarnished image, and the emotional drain of having to deal with a deservedly dissatisfied customer.

Emphasizing the long-term goal of creating positive relationships with lots of repeat purchases and/or referrals benefits the salesperson, the company, and the customer. From your perspective as the salesperson, it's both more rewarding and much easier to pursue prospects who are likely to remain on the conveyor belt for many repeat purchase cycles.

The company is much better off, too, as revenues that result from future repeat purchases are much more highly profit leveraged than are those from the first order. The high initial acquisition costs can be amortized over all future transactions, so the original marketing expenses, when spread over many sales, may become negligible. This allows a much higher proportion of the revenues to fall to the bottom line as profits.

Prospects also benefit by concentrating their buying relationships with the vendors who will serve as long-term partners. Think about your own experiences. Isn't it easier and more enjoyable to do business with vendors who have served you well for a long time?

The one area of sales and marketing that has traditionally received the most attention is that of closing the sale. In the context of bringing customer relationships to life, closing is not tricking, pressuring, or coercing a prospect into buying something. Instead, the focus is on opening a relationship. Prospecting and acquisition costs are usually much higher than are profit margins on initial sales. The profit-minded salesperson may even realize that it's better *not* to go to the trouble of getting customers on the conveyor belt discussed in Chapter 1— that is, unless they're likely to remain on it for many repeat purchases or renewals (and provide valuable referrals).

Shift your selling emphasis from closing sales to beginning, nurturing, and rekindling repeat buying and referring relationships.

W *hat you can do, starting NOW:*

- When your results are falling short, realign your thoughts, words, and actions using the CPR model.
- Begin your *consultations* with open-ended questions to make it easier for your prospects to reveal their needs.
- *Personalize* your benefits by matching them with your prospects' own statements about their needs.
- Always keep the powerful concept of *recommending* foremost in your thoughts and words.

14

WINNING EVEN
WHEN YOUR PROSPECT
SAYS "NO SALE"

What we'll cover in Chapter 14:

- Changing the way you look at failed calls and turning them into beneficial, profitable experiences
- Gaining referrals, even from noncustomers
- Salvaging sales by arranging future contacts
- Learning what went wrong from those who say "no"
- Ending unsuccessful calls positively for long-term payoffs

You may be phenomenally successful at preheating your prospects and may experience an amazing success rate of 60 percent! Or you may be more typical and experience success in the 10 to 20 percent range. Or maybe it's only 3 percent. Loads of factors influence your ability to be successful. The source of your leads, the competitive environment, your company's reputation, the value you offer, and, most important of all, your own preheating strategies and sales techniques when you're in dialogue with your prospect— all have an impact on your ability to succeed.

The statistics I've just mentioned are based on my broad experiences with salespeople working in a wide range of industries. Of course, the numbers aren't exactly right for your specific sales situation, but one thing I know for sure is that you're not going to have 100 percent success. Somewhere between 40 percent and 97 percent of the time, you're going to fail. But wait a minute, is that accurate? If your call doesn't conclude with a prospect saying yes! have you really *failed?* Certainly not. At the very, very least, you will have discovered an approach that didn't work.

FAILURE MEANS ONLY "NO SALE AT THIS TIME WITH THIS PROSPECT"

Throughout this book, I've regularly repeated my focus on the connections between our actions, our thoughts, and our words. When you describe and think of a no-sale call as a failure, you rob yourself of the ability to gain from the experience. There are lots of ways to benefit in this situation, as I'll detail below. The most important starting point is to adjust your thinking and your vocabulary.

Becoming outstanding at preheating prospects and opening long-term buying relationships with them is an ongoing process. Every call that isn't successful can still yield valuable information about what you should do differently next time. As you'll see in Chapter 16, I recommend that you periodically and randomly sit down and carefully analyze what prevented you from achieving the outcome you wanted. Aside from the psychological benefit of reframing your thinking and vocabulary and viewing each failed call as a learning opportunity, there are also significant tangible benefits to be realized even when the prospect says no!

All you can really say for sure is that this particular prospect did not respond affirmatively to this particular offer presented in this particular way at this particular time.

WHY YOU SHOULD ALWAYS ASK FOR REFERRALS, EVEN FROM NONPROSPECTS

It may be that a prospect said no because his or her set of needs simply didn't match up well with the benefits you can offer at this time. If you're selling discounted air freight services and the shipping department manager you've talked with doesn't buy from you, that may be simply because all the company's shipments are local and delivered by truck. If you're talking with a Kansas-based manufacturer of cardboard packaging materials whose customer base is located in Kansas, of course it's not going to buy air courier services from you. (It also suggests that you need a better-qualified prospect list to work from!)

Because of the way the preheating call is structured, you'll realize that early on in the conversation, because you've asked your open-ended and multiple-choice discovery questions. It would be idiotic for you to continue and attempt to close a sale when the prospect doesn't need what you offer. But wait, don't hang up yet. This prospect may still be a good source for referrals, even though he or she is not a candidate for your services:

> "Mr. Sarlo, it's pretty clear that your product category and marketing area mean you're unlikely to need the specialized air freight services we offer. Still, you may be a member of an organization for logistics managers or may have friends and associates whose companies could benefit from our services. Which of your

colleagues have expanded into market areas that I may be able to help with?"

KNOWING WHEN TO SUGGEST FUTURE CONTACT

Remember one important part of the verbal reframing I suggested at the outset: ". . . at this time. . . ." There may well be certain timing factors that stand in the way of beginning a purchasing relationship right now but may not be an obstacle later.

Many insurance companies call on me to train their personnel in how to sell more effectively. Some of these companies specialize in preferred automobile insurance, stipulating that new customers must have a clean record during the last three years with no moving violations or insurance claims (although underwriting requirements vary from company to company). Perhaps the prospect you're speaking with received a speeding ticket two and a half years ago and thus would not qualify for coverage. In the process of discussing this potential policyholder's overall situation, you discover his record by running a standard report offered by your state's motor vehicle department. Sure enough, the citation shows up, and you'll know that this person doesn't qualify for coverage, which doesn't mean you should abandon your efforts, though. Simply explain the situation and let your prospect know that you can likely help him save significantly on his insurance premiums by securing coverage six months later, when the citation no longer appears in his three-year driving history. Agree to schedule a follow-up call at that time.

LEARN FROM YOUR BEST MARKET RESEARCHERS: PEOPLE WHO SAY NO!

People who say no usually do so for a very good reason. They know what the reason is, and it may involve something about the approach you've used with them. Why not ask what turned them away?

"Mr. Drange, I'll certainly respect your decision not to transfer your auto insurance at this time. There's one last thing I would appreciate your help with. As we've been talking about your situation, it's clear to *me* that you would save a lot on your premiums and would get superior coverage by making the move. So there must be something I haven't explained clearly enough, or perhaps there's something about my approach that has put you off a bit. I'd be very grateful if you'd help me understand what I can do to improve. I want to help people like you take advantage of this preferred coverage; if there's something about my approach that gets in the way, and I'm not even aware of it, I'm doing people like you a disservice. Don't worry about hurting my feelings. Please tell me what I could have done better to explain the benefits of this preferred coverage."

Consider the possible outcomes of this approach. For one, you may well learn that there's something about your technique that rubbed this prospect the wrong way. If you can impress on him that you really do want to know, he may just open up and tell you. You may hear something critical about your style or manner that others have also been noticing but not telling you about. If you can clean up just one little habit that will help you eliminate obstacles for others in future calls, you'll come out way ahead. It may also be that this additional probing reveals that your prospect's reluctance has nothing to do with your particular approach. Instead, there may be a possible misunderstanding about what you're offering. If you can get the dialogue going, you'll find out what's been misunderstood, and you might just turn this person around after all. Even if you don't get the sale or learn something that will improve your future approaches, you will at the very, very least have left this prospect feeling more positive about you and your company.

People like to deal with those who are continually seeking to improve themselves. Let's not overlook the personal benefit you'll gain. As a sales professional, you will think more highly of yourself by knowing you're on a path of continual improvement, and that will help you present yourself more positively to the next prospect.

LEAVE YOUR PROSPECTS FEELING GOOD

I've been in situations, and I'll bet you have been too, when a salesperson senses that he or she won't be successful at closing a sale with you and exits from the call hurriedly or even rudely. Haven't you had solicitors hang up on you? It leaves a bad taste in your mouth, a hostile attitude toward future callers, and it certainly tarnishes the calling company's reputation. Think of it this way: your telephone contact with a prospect represents the culmination of a very costly set of steps. You or your company have invested time and money in acquiring the lead, prequalifying it, and taking some steps to preheat the prospect (perhaps by e-mails and/or other mailings), and now you've invested the time to make telephone contact, perhaps after several missed attempts, voice mail messages, and so on. After all this, doesn't it make good sense to invest just a few extra seconds to ensure that the call ends on a positive note? You end up feeling better about your work, leaving this prospect receptive to future calls and helping to blunt negative word-of-mouth publicity in the marketplace.

"Mrs. Drange, thank you for considering our insurance. I'm sorry that it wasn't quite right for you at this time. I've appreciated your courtesy on the phone and have enjoyed talking with you. I wish you many years of safe driving and will be happy to be of service in the future."

That took just about 15 seconds. Isn't the investment in goodwill and personal pride worth it?

SIMPLE FOLLOW-THROUGH STEPS THAT TAKE YOUR PROSPECTS BY SURPRISE

Even better, you can cap off the experience just described by sending a thank-you note to your prospect. Enclose some of your business cards. Ask for referrals. Offer to be of service in the future. It's a very small additional investment considering the efforts you've already made and gives you the opportunity to secure future business while creating goodwill in the marketplace and making yourself feel good too.

Make Prospects Feel Glad You Refer Them Elsewhere

In some instances, you won't want to move forward, even if the prospect does. I'm definitely not saying that you should ignore prospects or slam down the phone if unqualified leads don't answer your questions in a way that makes you think you have a shot at building a long-term relationship.

When you tell a prospect "no" because her needs are not a good fit with your products or services, make sure you do it in a way that leaves her feeling good about having been in contact with you. Suppose you sell roofing services, and this prospect's needs aren't up your alley; you specialize in flat roof commercial torch-down systems, but this prospect needs her cedar shake roof redone. It's not going to sound too good if you say, "Look, I'm not going to waste my time on you, because I'm not going to end up with the job anyway." Instead, phrase your wish to decline in positive terms:

"Mrs. Hunsaker, based on what you're telling me about your needs, I'm not the roofer who's best suited to help you. Rather than take up your time and attention by having you meet with me, let me make a couple of suggestions and steer you toward somebody who specializes in your kind of project. I know several qualified cedar shake roofing specialists, and I'll be glad to give you their numbers."

Then offer the referrals. You'll benefit from the professional courtesy by forging stronger relationships with your roofing colleagues, and those relationships in turn are likely to result in referrals to you from them when they come across prospects who are just right for your specialty. But even more important, you will have done the right thing for the prospect. I'm personally convinced that's always your best course of action.

Attempting to sell your product or service to someone who isn't likely to be happy over the long haul is only going to bring you and your prospect dissatisfaction and discord. Oh, I realize some readers will laugh at this paragraph and say, "Are you kidding? I'm going to take any sale I can get, and then get outta there!" But I choose to believe that their numbers are small and they aren't going to succeed in the long run anyway. Ethical businesspeople who put their prospects' needs first win in the long run.

GETTING QUALIFIED LEADS FROM UNQUALIFIED PROSPECTS

When you tell prospects that what you sell doesn't fit well with what they need and then proceed to help them with a referral, you're ideally positioned to ask them for *their* referrals. In the roofing example, it would be entirely appropriate to continue and say:

"The three roofers I've suggested are all well qualified, and I'm sure you'll get the help you need for your cedar shake roof. My specialty, as I said, is commercial roofs, and it may be that you know someone who owns a commercial building. Although I'm not the best person to help you, I may be able to help one of your friends. Who are the two or three people who come to mind when you think of people involved with commercial properties?"

You've already demonstrated your sense of honor and have already invested the time to proceed this far in getting to know your prospect's needs. Leverage that investment by asking for qualified referrals.

If you're really interested in profits, your aim is not to make the maximum number of onetime sales. Invest the time to identify highly qualified prospects, those who may develop into long-term, repeat-purchase partners so that you can concentrate on providing a higher quality of sales attention to a smaller quantity of solid prospects.

What you can do, starting NOW:

- Change your vocabulary. Rather than saying "I failed," say, "This approach didn't work with this prospect at this time."
- Always ask for referrals, even when your prospect turns out not to be qualified.
- Ask for permission and arrange future contacts when you foresee changed circumstances.
- Enlist the assistance of prospects who decline by asking them how you can improve.
- Always invest the extra moments necessary to leave prospects feeling good about your contact.

15

PATCHING THE LEAKS IN YOUR SALES PIPELINE

The term *sales pipeline* is very common in the sales world. It's most often used in connection with a timing connotation. That is, the sales manager asks how your numbers are looking for the next quarter. You reply that you've "got a lot of business in the pipeline." That means you are developing leads into suspects into prospects into first-time buyers into long-term relationships. It's also a shorthand way of saying "I know my numbers aren't looking too good for this month, but I have a lot of new business in the pipeline, and my numbers for next month will be much better. Just wait until you see the good stuff that's coming down the pipeline."

YOUR BUSINESS FLOW DEPENDS ON YOUR DRIPS

I love to use props when dramatizing important concepts during my seminars and keynote presentations. I remember standing in front of an audience of industrial equipment salespeople and holding up a very odd contraption, a kind of plumber's nightmare. It looked like a section of the piping system from a house Dr. Seuss designed. A two-foot long section of three-inch diameter PVC piping led to a 45° angled elbow, which led to a bushing that reduced the diameter of the pipe from three inches to two inches. Then there was a two-inch T fitting with one of its three openings left unplugged and wide open. Along the entire length of this contraption, I had drilled holes of various sizes. Some were the size of a pencil, others mere pinholes, and still others gaping three-quarter-inch holes. If you were to get a funnel and pour a gallon of water into the big end of the pipe, barely a few drops would trickle out the other end.

I began this particular presentation by explaining that the company's sales management team had asked me to talk about "Pipeline Management." I had undertaken a thorough analysis of the company's current sales pipeline. The best way I could characterize it visually was with this kinky, leaky, messed-up contraption. You could put a lot of sales leads in at one end, but very few of them would come out the other end as new customers.

Everybody understands the notion that a chain is only as strong as its weakest link. My philosophy, when it comes to the sales pipeline, is quite similar: *Your sales pipeline is only as good as your biggest leak.*

Think of it this way: suppose your sales manager gives you a list of 100 (supposedly) qualified prospects. You enthusiastically slip on your telephone headset, grab your calling list, and start attempting to make contacts.

After calling all 100 contacts on the list, you've found that 35 simply can't be reached. These may be people who've changed jobs, the company has gone out of business, or whatever.

Of the 65 remaining valid prospects, you attempt to arrange callback appointments or leave messages, but 40 of those just simply don't work out; you never make contact.

Now we're down to 25 prospects with whom you may actually have a telephone conversation. But of those, odds are that at least 50 percent will be turned off for some reason during the initial contact, or you'll discover that they're definitely not qualified prospects after all. Now we're down to 12 or 13 possible prospects.

Let's say that about half of them are just plain not a good fit for the product or service you offer. So now we're down to a half dozen or so prospects with whom you may actually engage in a sales dialogue.

If your sales skills are superb, you may initiate a sale with 2 or 3 of them. So how did we get from the original 100 prospects down to just a couple of sales? Leaks!

FIND AND PATCH YOUR WORST LEAKS FIRST

The single best piece of advice I can offer to salespeople whose concentration is on winning new prospects and getting them on the relationship conveyor belt is to stop and think. It's easy to get so caught up in the activity that the activity itself seems to be the goal. When a sales manager asks, "How is your prospecting coming along?" the wrong answer is:

> "Great! I'm sending out hundreds of catalogs and brochures. I feel sure there's some good business waiting out there."

That response is representative of the *al dente* way of thinking I talked about in Chapter 1. If your aim were to stay busy and generate a large *quantity* of work rather than a significant *quality* of business, your boss would be pleased. But what you really want to do is thin out those poorly qualified suspects so you're able to focus your attention on the few who may actually develop into relationships.

A better response would be:

> "Great! I've had contact with most of my 100 current leads and have narrowed them down to about 25 who look like good prospects. I'm giving those 25 close personal attention and have sent a quick form letter to the other 75 who don't look so hot."

One of my clients is another large insurance company that constantly urges new agents to schedule as many sales appointments as possible. I created a custom video training program for the company that shows its agents how to be more persuasive at convincing suspects to set aside time to sit down for a personal meeting (they call appointments "sits"). My client was surprised when the call guides I prepared included an "out" that let agents *not* meet with prospects who showed little likelihood of eventually becoming policyholders. The results? Agents feel better about their work and don't waste time (nor suffer from lagging morale) meeting with people who just aren't going to buy. Instead, they concentrate their attention on doing a much better job of preparing for sales calls with real prospects and are more conscientious about their follow-up activities.

That probably sounds like it contradicts the traditional approach to selling. And it does. Traditional approaches are designed to produce quantity rather than quality. You don't want lots and lots of unqualified leads any more than you want lots and lots of unproductive appointments. The sooner you find out that a supposed prospect has a very slim chance of ever actually buying from you, the sooner you can shift your focus to those truly qualified prospects who deserve and want your concentrated, quality attention.

Do You Want Busyness or Business?

One primary source of your cold call prospecting list may be trade show leads. They're usually of dubious value, as you've probably discovered.

Steve Miller, trade show consultant and author of *How to Get the Most Out of Trade Shows* (NTC Business Books, 1990), points to the widespread misconception that an exhibitor's success can be measured by observing how crowded the booth is and by asking salespeople how busy they've been. Busy doesn't mean effective; in fact, there may be an inverse correlation between busyness and business. One of Steve's key challenges is showing companies how to be less busy and get more business. Average costs per trade show lead can run in the $400 to $500 range and sometimes up to $1,000. So we're talking about leveraging some very significant investments. Travel expenses for booth personnel, exorbitant shipping charges, fees to the trade show company, plant, carpet, and furniture rentals (and let's not forget those union guys who want $150 just to plug in your spotlights) really add up.

Weyerhaeuser's DRIpride adult diaper marketers, for example, are well represented at the American Healthcare Association's trade show each year. Administrators of extended-care facilities are prime sales prospects. Before Steve revamped his client's trade show plans, the client was delighted to generate nearly 2,000 leads from the show. The trouble was, the follow-up was dismal, and company insiders joked about the piles of business cards sitting on someone's desk back at headquarters. In the year when Steve guided the efforts, the number of leads gathered plunged by two-thirds to only 600. But these were quality prospects, who generated $6.5 million in documented sales within the next 90 days. The leads were far fewer in number but far higher in quality. As a result, they got attention rather than being added to some dusty pile.

Think about the benefits of making a similar revision to your own prospecting system. Be much more selective about qualifying leads and verifying both purchase intention and authority. What if you didn't frantically attempt to give equal attention to all of your leads, even though most will turn out to be not so highly qualified? Your most highly qualified prospects, those who are most deserving of your attention, would get more of it. Your frustration would be lowered because you wouldn't be spinning your wheels on low-quality prospects. The annoyance felt by your less-qualified prospects who aren't going to turn into long-term customer relationships anyway would be reduced. It benefits everyone to scale back your prospecting efforts so that you concentrate more quality attention on fewer (but higher-quality) prospects.

Steve instructs the personnel staffing his clients' trade show booths to ask direct, specific questions that will qualify the booth visitors immediately. If after asking four questions (to determine job title, buying authority, company size, and so forth, for example), you don't get four encouraging answers, Steve advises you to politely thank the visitor for stopping by, honestly explain that there probably isn't a good fit with what your company sells, and suggest that the visitor shouldn't waste his or her valuable time by lingering any longer.

You've been to plenty of trade shows at which exhibitors have a big fishbowl at their booth, and you're encouraged to drop in your card to qualify for some drawing or contest. U.S. Bank used the fishbowl technique to get leads at boat shows, hoping that some boat buyers would finance their yachts through the bank. The bank's booth personnel did succeed in getting hundreds of business cards but produced little traceable revenue. At the first boat show after Steve came on board, the fishbowl was gone. The bank's booth personnel made direct eye-to-eye contact with visitors, asked qualifying questions, and solicited cards from only 180 qualified leads willing to commit to a next step (meaning a quote, an office visit, or a completed loan application). U.S. Bank lost the fishbowl but gained $3 million in new loans within 30 days.

Your qualifying questions should always fall into the following four areas:

1. **Intent:** "Are you simply gathering information and shopping around at this point, or are you actually beginning the process of narrowing the field of potential suppliers and moving toward selecting one?"
2. **Timing:** "What's your most likely timing for this purchase? Are you planning to move forward in the next couple of months, later in the year, or well down the road?"
3. **Budget:** "Has the budget allocation for this purchase already been committed, or is it in early planning for your next fiscal year?"
4. **Authority:** "In addition to yourself, who else will be involved in making this decision? Is there a review committee involved, or is this a decision that *you're* going to be making?"

These four types of questions give you a very clear picture of just how serious a prospect you're really dealing with. If you're not hearing answers that suggest at least a reasonable likelihood you'll be able to secure the business, consider disqualifying the prospect rather than spinning your wheels.

I'm certainly not suggesting that you toss away potential customers who aren't quite chomping at the bit or who don't have sole purchasing authority. I *am* saying that you should trust your intuition. Almost always, your sales experience will lead you to a pretty accurate assessment of your prospects. When they're very remote, the best allocation of your energy and resources may result from disqualifying long-shot prospects.

Who Benefits When You Disqualify Prospects?

Saying no to people who really aren't qualified prospects benefits you as well as your current customers and your future customers. You and your organization may be squandering scarce resources by throwing pasta up on the ceiling (using the *al dente* prospecting technique mentioned in Chapter 1). Mailing expensive brochures, burdening the field salesforce with low-quality leads, and keeping the fulfillment clerks busy sending out costly stuff to people who aren't going to become repeat customers drains resources. Patching leaks and eliminating unqualified prospects early on means you'll be in a position to concentrate on the much more profitable tasks: focusing top-quality attention on your most qualified prospects, nurturing current relationships, and salvaging relationships that have gone awry.

Your current customers also benefit because they'll be the beneficiaries of that attention. Remember, they want more attention, and they value closer bonds with you.

Your future customers benefit, too. Rather than spinning your wheels and attending to marginally qualified suspects, you'll be concentrating quality attention on prospective buyers, helping them reach good decisions, and giving them the followup attention that will convert their single purchases into longterm, repeat buying relationships.

MY OWN QUALIFICATION SYSTEM

I used to send out information about my services as a keynote speaker to anyone who asked for it. There's a widespread belief in my profession that prospects may be scared off if they know your speaking fees before they've read your brochure, seen your video, and know your reputation. Many of my colleagues refuse to quote a fee in an initial conversation.

I've come to recognize that only a very small percentage of people who call and ask about my speeches and seminars are ever going to be in a position to hire me. I use my professional fee as an early step in the qualification process. I want prospects to know my fees before we even talk, so I've set up a page on my Web site that tells possible clients exactly what I charge for my services. If their budget is much smaller and we never connect, that's fine with me. We wouldn't have been able to work together anyhow. I dedicate my attention to my most qualified prospects.

When I do talk with prospects firsthand, I ask them exactly what they want their speaker to accomplish during the presentation. If I can't meet their goals, why would I want the assignment? I ask what other professional speakers a client has particularly enjoyed working with in the past. Because I know most of my top-tier speaking colleagues, their personal presentation style, and their fee, I get a very good idea of what will make this client happy. If we don't have a great fit, let's not work together! The client would just end up unhappy, and I'd end up refunding my fee.

I think of my follow-up mailings as $100 bills. A bona fide prospect will want to review my books, tapes, and videos as well as read my brochure, so the package I send contains a lot of valuable materials. But it's my attention that's worth the most to me. My estimate of a $100 cost per fulfilled inquiry is very conservative, considering the opportunity cost of my using my prospecting time to write another book or serve a current client. I don't like to throw away a lot of $100 bills, so I'm very careful to qualify prospects before agreeing to send out information.

You shouldn't want to make a sale to just anyone. You want to have new prospects who stand a good chance of becoming long-term clients and will buy again and again, provide referrals, and talk you up in the marketplace, helping to produce more long-term relationships. If one prospective client is likely to end up unhappy because your product or service wasn't really what he or she was looking for, you'll end up making an enemy who can do you great harm.

Think of your follow-up lead-fulfillment system as a way of dispensing cash. Maybe $100 is the wrong figure for you; perhaps your follow-up is worth only $50 or even only $20. (Or it may be $500!) Do you really want to squander a lot of $20 or $100 bills? If you're not going to pursue a semivalid lead quite vigorously, you're better off to not respond at all. Save your energy and resources for those few prospects who are worth handling right.

There is a risk that you'll overlook a few highly qualified prospects when you adopt more stringent qualification procedures. But there's a much greater risk that you and your organization will flounder in a sea of unqualified leads if you don't.

LEAKS AND KINKS!

Think back to the sales pipeline analogy and my big clumsy, kinky PVC piping contraption. Your goal, of course, is to have plenty of prospects emerging at the far end of your pipeline as new customers.

One of the smartest, most highly leveraged things you can do as a salesperson is go on a plumbing investigation. Identify where your prospects are leaking away.

Sometimes a huge leak has to do with your organization's systems rather than your own persuasive or interpersonal communication skills. For example, the industrial equipment company I was speaking for had an excellent advertising campaign that prompted prospective customers to reply and request a catalog and brochure. Sure enough, many did. Then the clerk who had been assigned to handle these leads wrote them out on little cards and bundled them with a large rubber band. Because the home office was so busy, these bundles of cards were sent off to the suburban branch offices, where they were treated as overflow work—that is, unless the branch office was also very busy.

Eventually, these supposedly hot leads were put into the computer system for access and follow-up by the salespeople. Unfortunately, this whole process took about five weeks. By the time the salesperson called the once-interested prospects, they had long since forgotten that they'd even responded. Even if they had remembered, they wouldn't be thinking very highly of the company. That amounts to a gusher of a leak.

Sometimes it's not really a gushing leak but more of a kink—something that just makes it difficult to engage in productive dialogue with your prospective customer. Suppose you hand out a business card or leave a phone message that includes the telephone number that reaches your company's receptionist. You're asking your prospect to go through the extra step of having a receptionist transfer the call to your extension. What happens if the prospect calls after hours when the receptionist isn't there to direct the call? Be honest now, do you find that you really *enjoy* spelling out the names of individuals you want to reach using one of those automated telephone attendant staff directories? The bottom line here is that you could eliminate that one small kink in the communication system by simply making sure that your extension number appears on your business cards and in phone messages.

Admittedly, adding your extension number to the phone contact section of your business card is not a big change and only makes a very slight difference. You're making it easier for just a few prospects to reach you. It won't even apply to many of them unless they call after hours when your switchboard is closed. However, consider this: Cumulatively speaking, one of the best ways to get more business flowing through your sales pipeline is to patch as many leaks as possible, even small ones. Although you will get your greatest benefit from patching your biggest leaks, always be on the alert for even the tiny little things that make it difficult or frustrating for your prospects. Each time you eliminate one little glitch . . . or leak . . . you're aiding the flow. Displaying a complete phone number next time you have business cards reprinted is like plugging up one of those small pinholes in the pipeline. Identifying why it takes more than a month for sales leads to reach you and fixing the situation is like plugging one of the gaping three-quarter-inch holes. Each time you patch a hole of any size, you're increasing the flow and making it easier to convert suspects into prospects into customers into relationships.

As you search for leaks in your own prospecting system, be sure to look in unexpected places, even though they may be right in front of your nose. I'm always surprised that advertisers persist in displaying their company Web site URLs using all lowercase letters. Haven't you squinted at advertising signs trying to figure out just what Web site they're directing you to? Consider the visual difference between: http://www.eradicatehungrymoles.com and http://www.EradicateHungryMoles.com, or http://www.thetastiesttortillasever.com and http://www.TheTastiestTortillasEver.com. The point of including your URL in advertising is to drive people to your Web site. If people can't figure out what it is, can't remember it, or can't accurately type it, they're not going to find you.

If the company you sell for expends many thousands of dollars to heighten prospects' awareness of your organization so that your calls are welcome, but the people they're advertising to can't readily decipher the URL, they're not going to recognize you when you call. So even though you may not do one single thing to improve your personal effectiveness on the phone, you're going to experience greater success if your company's URL is displayed in a way that makes your calls more welcome. Your e-mail address should be displayed the same way.

This is an example of a leak in your sales pipeline that might seem to be well outside your direct personal control. But that's just not the case. Because you care about producing great results and want to get as much business as you possibly can, take it upon yourself to find out who's responsible for your company's advertising and show that person or those persons how to do it better. Every leak you can patch helps.

We want to create a free-flowing pipeline, one where we don't lose leads because of huge leaks and one that encourages smooth and easy dialogue between you and your prospects. Always be alert for any kinks or leaks that interfere with a steady flow from suspects to prospects to new customers to lifetime relationships.

Suppose you have a smoothly functioning prospecting system, and you're even making use of good contact management software. Immediately following your calls, you're careful to make notes of what you discussed. But you're a slow, one-finger typist. If everything else about your follow-up system runs well, your typing speed amounts to a kink in your pipeline. It's an easy one to straighten out! I'm always surprised when professional salespeople type poorly. Because knowing how to type affects so many areas of your professional success, why not simply buy yourself one of the many inexpensive programs that teach you to type more quickly and accurately or buy and learn to use speech recognition software? It's a very simple step you can take that yields great benefits in your prospecting activities as well as in other areas of your life. Plugging every leak helps.

Heat Up Your Cold Calls is about building a prospecting and selling system that works more effectively so you can produce more results and reap bigger rewards from your efforts. Much of our concentration has been on your personal techniques: vocal adjustments, vocabulary changes, welcoming techniques, and so on. You still benefit, though, when you think of what you're doing as part of an overall system, and any steps you take to make the system run more smoothly produce benefits for you.

W*hat you can do, starting NOW:*

- Stop sending out all those costly fulfillment packages to unqualified prospects.
- Early in the qualification process, ask specific questions designed to reveal intent, timing, budget, and authority.
- Remember that your current customers benefit when you stop squandering attention on low-quality, poorly qualified prospective new customers.
- Make it as easy as possible for customers and prospects to reach you by adding your extension number every time you display your phone number.
- Wherever you show your e-mail address or company Web site URL, use mixed case text so it's easier to decipher and remember.
- Learn to type better and faster, or invest in speech recognition software.

WHERE DO WE GO FROM HERE?

You don't just read a book and wait for magic to happen. Implementing the strategies and tactics we've covered together takes a lot of work and time. You'll need to stay on track and continually work toward heating up your cold calls and making prospects listen, respond, and buy from you.

16

IS IT WORKING?
HOW TO TRACK YOUR
EFFECTIVENESS AND
BOOST YOUR ROI

What we'll cover in Chapter 16:

- Improving your return on investment by constantly monitoring the effectiveness of your strategies, techniques, and the specific words you use in conversations
- Why you should thoroughly analyze a random call every single day
- Tracking your improving effectiveness with a daily Personal Performance Assessment recapping your results
- Using your incoming solicitation calls as a test lab so you can gauge your reactions and incorporate them into your own sales approaches

Naturally, you're going to experience lots of ups and downs with your calling and selling success ratios. The aim of this book is to assist you in making sure that your trajectory is always upward. You have to know where you stand today compared with yesterday and last month in order to know that it's working. And that requires measurement. As you improve your effectiveness, you increase your ROI (return on investment).

THE CRUCIAL VALUE OF MEASURING AND MODIFYING YOUR APPROACH

There are lots of ways to get feedback about your effectiveness. If you work for a large company, ask about your organization's call-monitoring policies. If you work in a call center, supervisors and managers probably have the capability to privately monitor your calls. It has always seemed strange to me that some salespeople resent being "listened in on." If you work for a company where you don't believe the supervisory personnel are there to help, maybe you should change employers! Theoretically, at least, these are people with training and expertise, and they've seen many others before you use successful and not-so-successful techniques. Don't wait for them to critique your calls; go seek their feedback. At the very least, audiotape your own half of your conversations and critique yourself.

Becoming aware of your own shortcomings is one of the most important steps in changing them. In Chapter 5, we reviewed a whole list of words and phrases that can interfere with your effectiveness on the phone. You may readily agree that saying "I'll have to . . ." projects a less positive image than you'd really like to put across. Accepting that and believing it is one thing. Actually eliminating the phrase from your vocabulary is a whole different matter. When you record your own conversations, you give yourself the ability to look over your own shoulder. Ask your colleagues to help too.

When You Should Evaluate Your Results

The simple answer is *constantly!* I'm going to suggest two structured ways for you to evaluate your own performance. But first I suggest that you take a moment of introspection after every single call you make, regardless of the outcome. Ask yourself, "What did I say immediately before that last prospect either agreed to move forward or gave me a negative response?" Let's say that for the next ten calls your prospects respond "no" when you ask, "Would you like to consider scheduling a face-to-face appointment?" By paying attention to a series of such negative results, you get the idea that maybe *that* particular form of your question isn't going to produce the affirmative answers you're after. So you experiment with changing it. Try it another way: "I *recommend* that we meet briefly toward the end of the week. Is Thursday or Friday more convenient for you?" You use that approach for the next few calls and bingo! You notice that you start getting affirmative responses. So you change what you're doing and experience improved results. I know this sounds awfully basic and obvious, yet the reality is that most people get stuck in a rut and keep saying the same thing again and again, even though it's not producing the results they want.

THE DAILY RANDOM POSTCALL ANALYSIS

Take a look at the Postcall Analysis Form I've included on page 174. I invite you to download a full-size PDF version by visiting this book's Web site: http://www.HeatUpYourColdCalls .com. You're welcome to duplicate and use this copyrighted form, provided that it's strictly for your personal use.

You know that old story about the two wood choppers working side by side? One chops away furiously, making slow headway and becoming very exhausted because his axe is dull. The second asks the first one why he doesn't stop and sharpen it.

POST-CALL ANALYSIS _____

Did you achieve your Primary Objective?

Why? _____

Why not? _____

What specific words got a "YES"/"NO"? _____

_____

What could have changed the outcome? _____

_____

Did you achieve your Secondary Objective?

Why? _____

Why not? _____

What specific words got a "YES"/"NO"? _____

_____

What could have changed the outcome? _____

_____

Did you ask for referrals?

Why? _____

Why not? _____

What specific words got a "YES"/"NO"? _____

_____

What could have changed the outcome? _____

_____

Overall, what did you do especially well? What needed improvement?

Consider:

Voice

Delivery

Objection Handling

Closing Technique

Benefits

Probing Questions

What ONE thing will you do differently on the next call?

_____

The first woodcutter replies that he's got far too much wood to chop and doesn't have the time.

You're also "chopping wood" as you prospect, and it's certainly worth your time to stop and "sharpen your axe" periodically. I recommend that you pick a random number at the start of your calling period. Decide that you're going to stop what you're doing and go through a careful analysis of that particular call. Let's say you pick the seventh call. It's important that you establish this random number up front; otherwise, it's far too tempting to stop and analyze a particularly successful call. You want to get a realistic picture of your *typical* call.

Now look at the five sections of the form on page 174.

- Earlier, in Chapter 6, we identified why it's so important to have more than one objective for any given call. Perhaps your primary objective was to schedule a specific, firm appointment date and time to meet with this prospect. So be honest. Did you get your appointment? Why or why not? What do your gut instincts tell you that you might have done slightly differently to achieve a better outcome?

- You should also have had a secondary objective. Even if you weren't successful at scheduling the appointment or consummating the sale, maybe you wanted to make sure that you at least got some helpful feedback. Did you get it? Why not?

- Referrals are so important that it's worth reminding yourself any time you analyze your efforts.

- The point of this exercise is not to beat yourself up. Identify what you did well and single out those areas in which you fell a little short and can improve. This is a totally personal exercise you're going through, so there's no reason to be anything other than completely honest. Be sure to give yourself credit for what you did well.

- Even if the opportunities for improvement are overwhelming, identify one single area you will focus on during your very next call. Then build on that momentum by making it a matter of daily habit in your future calls.

Personal Assessments That Keep You on Track . . . and Improving

Now look at the Personal Performance Assessment Sample Form on page 177. Again, I invite you to visit http://www .HeatUpYourColdCalls.com to download a full-size PDF and duplicate it for your personal use. As you'll see, a major focus of this form is identifying the gaps between yesterday's actual performance and today's performance compared with your goal, and setting a realistic goal for tomorrow.

Now shift your attention to the "Show Percentages" section of the form. Naturally, you'd like all of your prospects to say "yes" and proceed to schedule an appointment with you or agree to make a purchase. But there is something that's worse than getting a "no." And that's making no headway at all. You're much better off to determine that your prospect is definitely not a candidate for future attention than you are to have a prospect string you along without having made any decision. Depending on what you sell, it may take several calls and contacts, and even a series of appointments, before you consummate an actual sale. So with each call you should have a specific objective that moves your prospect forward in the decision process. Did your prospect take a step forward or not?

If your honest assessment results in a large percentage number in the "???" box, that assessment has two big negative effects: First, if you're dealing with a prospect who simply can't make a decision to move forward, you are squandering your time with that individual and robbing other, valid, capable-of-making-a-decision prospects of your attention. Second, you're also interfering with your own personal evaluation of your effectiveness. There's nothing wrong with having a prospect decide not to do

PERSONAL PERFORMANCE ASSESSMENT

Name: _____   Date: _____

	Yesterday ACTUAL	Today GOAL	Today ACTUAL	Tomorrow GOAL
Total Completed Calls				
Total Number of Calls				
Total Revenue				
Calls per Sale				
Average Order Size				
Dollars per Dial				

Show Percentages: [____] YES   [____] ???   [____] NO

The main reason that I did/didn't reach my goals today is that:

On about _____ % of today's calls, I didn't ask for the order.

On about _____ % of today's calls, I didn't try to cross-sell.

On about _____ % of today's calls, I didn't ask for an upgrade.

On about _____ % of today's calls, I didn't ask for referrals.

Today, I did an especially good job of: _____

_____

I need to work harder on: _____

_____

All day tomorrow, I will focus on improving my: _____

_____

business with you. You know that feeling of being strung along by prospects who seem to stall and put you off interminably. They bog down your follow-up system, prevent you from helping prospects who would truly benefit from the product or service you offer, and undermine your self-confidence.

In Chapters 8 and 13 we looked at the benefits of using open-ended and multiple-choice questions. There is also a value in asking yes/no questions in this one specific situation, which certainly isn't the most effective way of getting people to accept your proposition. However, when you sense that a prospective customer really has no intention of buying from you or meeting with you and is just stringing you along, ask a direct question to find out exactly where you stand:

> "Mrs. Peterson, I can certainly appreciate that a decision to switch research providers from your current source to our service is a complex decision. Over the last three months, we've had several conversations about your making such a change, and I've been happy to provide all the support materials you requested. I know you've talked about this in a couple of your committee meetings, yet I've apparently not been as successful as I'd like to be in demonstrating why the change would make sense for you. Even though I believe that our research services are just what you need, there may also be some other factors I don't understand that might interfere with your decision. To make sure I'm not wasting your time, and to be sure that I'm providing attention to those new customers who really do want to take advantage of our research services, let me just ask you directly, do you see yourself making the switch in the next month or two, or not?"

Perhaps Mrs. Peterson will say:

"Well, actually, there's some kind of personal relationship involved, and I'm encountering what seems to be committee resistance that I can't change. So the truth is, I don't think we will be changing to your service."

Wonderful! Oh, I know you'd much rather hear a "yes," but at least you're much better off knowing exactly where you stand. You're not going to make every sale. If this is one that can't be made, aren't you better off to move ahead and begin dealing with prospects whom you really do have a shot at winning over?

I'm a big fan of realistic honesty. No matter how good you are, some prospects will never agree to do business with you. There may be lots of other factors involved, including many which are outside your control. If that's reality, accept it! Move on. Don't get bogged down. You have an opportunity, and indeed a responsibility, to be of service to prospects who can really take advantage of what you offer.

HOW TO MONITOR THE KEY MEASUREMENT: DOLLARS PER DIAL

One of your fundamental aims in business is to be well compensated, and one primary aim of this book is to make sure that you are well rewarded for your efforts. The time, energy, and attention you dedicate to this profession are your investments. Is your return growing? One key way to measure your effectiveness is to identify how many times you've dialed your phone and then measure the results you've gained from doing so. This bottom-line measurement takes into account your effectiveness at reaching prospects, your persuasiveness during the call, your consistent use of upgrading and cross-selling techniques, and your ability to ask for referrals. For example, if you're really good at asking for referrals, it's going to take you far fewer dials to generate more bucks. This summary measurement gives an overall indication of your efficiency and effectiveness combined.

THE COLD CALLS YOU RECEIVE CAN BE YOUR BEST TEACHERS

Let your own experiences as a prospect be your teacher. As we go through life, we're being sold to. We're customers. We're reacting like customers. We're responding positively to some approaches and rejecting others. In fact, you might just think of your daily life and the inevitable encounters with other salespeople as your Cold Calling University of Higher Learning.

As I was preparing this manuscript, I made it a point to remain open to every incoming cold call. Many were just dreadful, and based on them I've crafted some of the "don't do this!" examples used earlier in the book.

Other cold calls, even some that were unsuccessful, ended up as "do this" examples I've used here. In every case, when I receive a cold call or any type of sales solicitation, I pay attention. What techniques did the salesperson use that worked on me? What turned me off? (Don't you notice, as I do, that whenever you receive an unexpected telephone call—and it's often in the evening—and hear a voice you don't recognize saying, "Good evening, Mr. Walther, how are you doing tonight?" you know right away that it's some sort of sales call? So why do salespeople keep using that technique?)

One such call I received while I was writing this book ended up being unsuccessful so far as the caller's original objectives were concerned but ultimately had a much greater payoff. It was not your typical sloppy cold call.

From out of the blue, I received an e-mail from an individual whose name I didn't recognize: Kieran Bird. The e-mail message started right off by prominently mentioning the name of my friend, fellow speaker, and author Brian Tracy. Because Brian and I have known and respected each other for years and both have had our audio programs published by Nightingale-Conant, this "implied endorsement from a mutual friend" caught my attention.

The e-mail concluded with a presumptive appointment. The sender, Kieran Bird, wrote that he would ". . . phone to follow-up on this offer on June 1. If the date doesn't work for you please call 800-555-1234 to arrange a time and day. Thank you."

Kieran phoned just as he said he would, and, predictably, I had not really given much attention to his written proposal. In essence, he wanted to sell me a supply of limited edition hard-back copies of a new book he was bringing to market in exchange for earning a significant commission on all my sales of his work. I knew right away that I was not interested in any such arrangement. However, in my quick initial scan of the first promotional e-mail, I felt a little concerned because I saw mention of "cold calling" in the text. I thought this might be a competing author whose promotion could somehow interfere with the success of my own book.

I put him off and told him that I'd get to it in the next few days. He offered to send me some sample chapters from his book via an e-mail attachment and then made a personal comment that caught my attention. Almost in passing, he made reference to something about my Web site and mentioned my daughter by name. In fact, there is a rather deeply buried page at http://www.GeorgeWalther.com with a picture and narrative about my daughter's life. (After all, she's a primary focus of *my* life.)

Kieran didn't say, "By the way, I'd like you to know that I've taken the trouble to do some research about you before calling." Instead, he just casually let it slip that he had done his homework. I noticed that I, as his prospect, had a positive reaction to this approach. I liked the subtlety and his lack of self-serving boastfulness. "OK," I thought to myself, "maybe I'd better give some attention to this guy."

I agreed that I'd talk with him the following week. He took it upon himself to contact my executive assistant and make reference to our prior conversation. Then he set a presumptive appointment that was date and time specific. My assistant has full authority to schedule phone calls for me, and she's also highly protective. Something about Kieran's approach when he talked with her tipped off her intuition and signaled that I would end up appreciating any time she'd schedule for me to talk with him.

Kieran had listened to and respected my assistant's suggestion that I be the one to place the call. (Recall from Chapter 6 that the person who places the call always has a significant advantage in terms of turf control.)

I phoned right on time. Or, to be more accurate, I phoned 30 seconds in advance of our appointed time. I would have been willing to bet that Kieran would be prepared and waiting for my call. Everything about this guy's marketing effort so far had impressed me that he was a salesperson who did things right. Because I had phoned that half minute early, we began our conversation with some friendly banter about my atomic clock. (OK, I admit it, I'm a little compulsive about things sometimes.)

I began to query Kieran about his publishing plans and some of his claims of previous successes. In every case, he answered directly and honestly without dodging or sidestepping my concerns.

I'd wager that Kieran probably had a pretty good idea that I wasn't going to go for it from early on in the call. Yet he gave no sign of being argumentative or of contesting my objections. He welcomed them. He remained open-minded. This flexible thinking let him be open to more than one desirable outcome from the call.

Every time I offered something that an ordinary salesperson might've interpreted as an objection or criticism, Kieran thanked me for making my point. He expressed appreciation throughout the call. In very short order, I determined that this was a gracious person with a very cooperative attitude.

In the end, I didn't agree to purchase and resell any of his books. However, something much better happened. I made a connection with someone whose personality I enjoyed and with whom I may nurture a mutually beneficial relationship in the future. There's a lot I can do to help Kieran, and there are doubtless some ways that he can help me. For starters I recommend that you acquire Kieran Bird's new book *PersonaPR: The End of the Cold Call Era.*

Kieran's own cold call to me embodied many of the techniques I'd written about earlier in *Heat Up Your Cold Calls,* and it also offered some great lessons. Let's recap them together:

- Pave the way for your phone call with another medium. One excellent approach, if you can get through the security filters, is to send an e-mail introducing yourself and the reason for your call.
- Use a named mutual connection whenever possible. Even if this is simply an implied endorsement, it certainly helps to make your prospect feel more receptive.
- Always set a presumptive appointment for your call. By stating that he would call on June 1 and then actually calling on the date he'd specified, Kieran impressed me as someone who follows through and actually does what he says he'll do.
- Let your advance research "leak out." Be confident that the time you've invested to become familiar with your prospect will have an immediate payoff in terms of enhancing your self-confidence during the call. On top of that, your prospect will sense that you've done your research without your having to blatantly say so.
- Remain gracious; never seek to make your prospect feel guilty.

- Set a hierarchy of objectives for your call and remain open-minded about the benefits you may receive and may impart, even though you may not consummate the sale.
- Always close on a strongly positive note. At the end of our call, Kieran was gracious and appreciative and made sure the last words I heard from him were "Thank you."

W *hat you can do, starting NOW:*

- Seek out call-monitoring opportunities from your supervisory team.
- Make note of the specific words you used just prior to sales approaches that are both successful and unsuccessful.
- Visit the http://www.HeatUpYourColdCalls.com Web site and download (and then use!) full-size copies of the Postcall Analysis Form and the Personal Performance Assessment Form.
- Adopt the goal of minimizing the number of undecided prospects. Find out where they stand and allocate your sales attention accordingly.
- Every time you receive a solicitation call, use it to notice the techniques that do and don't work on you. Modify your own sales approach accordingly.

17

TAKE YOUR NEXT STEPS

Just as you didn't stop your prospecting activities to read this book, neither did you forget that the process of improving your results is an ongoing one. I have prepared a special online appendix for you and keep it updated with the latest resources to help you put the principles you read about here into practice.

Visit http://www.HeatUpYourColdCalls.com for the latest resources on:

- Links to government Web sites showing the cold calling legislation applicable in your area
- Commercial enterprises that can assist you with "scrubbing" your prospecting list against the Do Not Call Registry
- Professional trade associations that offer conventions and educational forums to keep you up to speed
- Vendors who can help you with the creation and distribution of customized postcards

- Full-sized examples of the three forms included in these pages: Call Planner, Postcall Analysis, and Personal Performance Assessment

I always welcome your feedback about my work and about your own successful preheating strategies. Please contact me at:

George R. Walther, Speaking from Experience, Inc., 6947 Coal Creek Parkway SE #100, Newcastle (Seattle suburb), WA 98059; Telephone: 425-255-2900, Fax: 425-235-6360; Web site: http://www.GeorgeWalther.com.

I'm keenly interested in crafting a customized keynote presentation or training seminar for your company. I want to help you and your colleagues succeed . . . and have more fun doing it.

Index

Share the message!

Bulk discounts
Discounts start at only 10 copies and range from 30% to 55% off retail price based on quantity.

Custom publishing
Private label a cover with your organization's name and logo. Or, tailor information to your needs with a custom pamphlet that highlights specific chapters.

Ancillaries
Workshop outlines, videos, and other products are available on select titles.

Dynamic speakers
Engaging authors are available to share their expertise and insight at your event.

Call Dearborn Trade Special Sales at 1-800-621-9621, ext. 4444, or e-mail trade@dearborn.com.

Dearborn™
Trade Publishing
A **Kaplan Professional** Company